WILDSAM

"The world was peopled
with wonders."

The origin of Wildsam comes from above, a
line of prose in the novel *East of Eden*, written by
John Steinbeck. Six words hinting at a broad and
interwoven idea. One of curiosity, connection, joy. And
the belief that stories have the power to unearth the
mysteries of a place—for anyone. The book in
your hands is rooted in such things.

WILDSAM

Our thanks go out to all the folks who make Newport a thriving modern port as well as such a historical treasure trove. We received kind assistance from Kendra Smith, Audrey Finocchiaro, Bill Taveres of The Preservation Society of Newport County and many others. Race you to the nearest Del's.

WILDSAM FIELD GUIDES™

Copyright © 2023

All rights reserved. No portion of this book may be reproduced in any form without permission from the publisher.

Published in the United States by Wildsam Field Guides, Austin, Texas.

ISBN 978-1-4671-9987-2

Illustrations by Andrew Desforges

To find more field guides, please visit www.wildsam.com

CONTENTS

*Discover the people and places
that tell the story of Newport*

ESSENTIALS 008

*Trusted intel and travel info about iconic
places and important topics*

BESTS 015

*Selected recommendations for the most
authentic Newport experiences*

ALMANAC 023

*Archival excerpts, timelines, clippings
and other historical musings*

MAPS 045

*Illustrated renderings of subject matter
vital to the town's heart and soul*

INTERVIEWS 059

*Concise and meaningful one-way conversations
with locals of note*

STORIES 075

*Essays and poems exploring the town and its
surroundings from respected Newport writers*

INDEX 093

NOTES 096

WELCOME

AMONG ALL NEWPORT'S FACETS, the most startling is simple: Can this town really be so small? Just 11 square miles?

True—from a gull's-eye view, Newport is a mere fragment of territory, a tiny J-shaped pendant in New England's necklace of isles, peninsulas, straits and bays. Alight here for a spell, though, and the perspective shifts. To settle in Newport—for a summer, or a lifetime—is to immerse yourself in a vast world, today's glimmer reflecting a deep and briny past.

Stories knit together here like sailor's knots. One century binds to another. In Newport's mixed-up timelines, Pete Seeger and Joan Baez sing out on the Folk Festival stage as Vanderbilts and Astors and Kennedys flock to grand "cottages" on Bellevue Avenue. In reality as we know it now, this harbor comes alive in a wash of schooners, sunscreen and Del's Frozen Lemonade, Thames Street teeming with life at all hours.

Geography, of course, is so often destiny. Newport's specific arc between waters makes it a valued port, and many essentials—from pirate lore to America's Cup—flow from that. But there are many ports. A particular human magic thrives here, a complex, playful joy that spurs creativity and seeks lightness. This spirit works across time and the social spectrum. Bygone ladies meet for luncheon and gossip at the Casino. Bob Dylan plugs in his guitar and says, Well, how about *this*? Lawn tennis and polo share a town with gritty Sunset Leaguers at Cardines Field. Newport sojourners sketched the rules of croquet and started America's greatest bicycle club, while ornamenting the town with mansions overflowing with artistry.

To meet the Newporters of today is to meet people invested in every side of this town, all its many tales. Summer Newport is preppy and sentimental and zany. Then there's the sleepier, saltier side of things: Secret beaches, once-smoky dive bars. The steadfast Fifth Ward. Sunset drives to Brenton Point. Gatherings of Narragansett Nation members at Four Winds Community Center. Stories of enslaved and free Black people who built this city, as told by the 1696 Heritage Group. Long a beacon for those seeking sun and sea, Newport shows promise as a haven for all.

Newport is indeed humble in size on the map. But its soul, this town is immense. Within jus 11 miles, you can chart paths without limit.
—The Editors

ESSENTIALS

LANDMARKS

Touro Synagogue
Oldest synagogue in the U.S., completed 1763.

Redwood Library and Athenaeum
Enlightenment institution of colonial America.

Chinese Tea House
Alva Belmont's suffragist meeting house, now a brunch spot.

GREENSPACE

Fort Adams State Park
Former U.S. Army post, today a hub for sailing, fishing, picnicking and sports. Summertime spot for Jazz and Folk Fests.

MEDIA

RADIO
Preservation Society Newport County Hour
Deep dive into Newport mansions on 1540 AM. Guests include all manner of preservation folk.

NEWSPAPER
Newport Daily News
Full report, politics to culture.

BLOG
What's Up Newp
Local happenings from reliable sources.

ITINERARY

Morning. Breakfast at Belle's Café, followed by a stroll down Thames Street with window shopping.
Midday. Grab an iced coffee and a sandwich to go from The Nitro Bar. Swim and sun at Second Beach with a picnic lunch. Order a frosty treat at the Del's Lemonade truck.
Evening. Dinner at TSK. Digestif at Clarke Cooke House. Boom Boom Room for dancing that takes it late night.

FOODWAY

Awful Awful
A Rhode Island classic, made by blending ice milk [typically ice cream + milk] and flavored syrup. First served at Newport Creamery in the 1950s, this frosty treat was named by a customer who called it "awful big and awful good." Historically, the coffee version of this was known statewide as a Coffee Cabinet. Use Autocrat coffee syrup to whip up a caffeinated shake at home, or simply stir it into coffee milk.

MUSEUM

Newport Art Museum
Collection ranges from paper works to glass sculptures, 18th century to the present.

LODGING

Castle Hill Inn
Forty acres of historic luxury estate with ocean views. Private beaches, manicured lawns.

The Vanderbilt
Downtown mansion with modern glam touches. Charming decor, eccentric furnishings.

Hotel Viking
Vintage romance in a 100-year-old building. Gilded Age aura, wharfside dining and spa. Pretty much dead-center of town.

Captain Carl
Houseboat rental out of Newport Harbor. Cozy space for four, with galley kitchen.

Chart House Inn
Nostalgia meets novelty. Seven rooms and suites named after monumental Rhode Island women.

The Gardiner
A fresh effort with serious local roots champions Newport's artistic and creative heritage.

CULTURE

BOOKS

▷ *The Age of Innocence* by Edith Wharton: A Gilded Age love story among New York's elite, by the first woman to win a Pulitzer Prize.

▷ *Theophilus North* by Thornton Wilder: Semi-autobiographical tale of one man's experience in Newport's high society, circa 1926.

MUSIC

▷ *Newport Folk Festival 1963: The Evening Concerts, Vol. 1*: Live recordings: Joan Baez, Bob Dylan and The Freedom Singers' "We Shall Overcome."

▷ *Nina Simone at Newport*: The iconic jazz singer and songwriter, recorded live at the 1960 Newport Jazz Festival.

FILM

▷ *The Great Gatsby* [1974]: Robert Redford and Mia Farrow haunt Newport in an adaptation of F. Scott Fitzgerald's 1920s society novel.

▷ *Moonrise Kingdom*: Wes Anderson's colorful coming-of-age adventure with a retro-outdoorsy look, filmed on location in and around town.

HISTORY

Home to the Narragansett and Wampanoag tribes, Aquidneck Island attracted English settlers seeking religious freedom. Newport evolved into a hub for trade, the arts and the American leisure class.

1636.... Narragansett chiefs Canonicus and Miantonomi sign the deed for Aquidneck over to William Coddington

1638 ... Anne Hutchinson leads first English settlers to Aquidneck Island. After disputes, Coddington and Nicholas Easton move south to form Newport the following year.

1658 ... First wave of Jewish immigrants arrive in Newport

1675 ... Indigenous inhabitants fight New England colonists and their Indigenous allies in King Philip's War—one of the bloodiest conflicts per capita in North American history

1696 ... First documented ship carrying enslaved Africans to Rhode Island, *The Seaflower*, arrives in Newport

1776 ... Revolution-era British occupation of Newport begins; lasts until 1779

1839.... Kingscote built on Bellevue Avenue: early lavish "summer cottage"

1851 ... Construction begins on Chateau-sur-Mer, now seen as curtain-raiser to the Gilded Age

1854 ... Newport Historical Society founded

1875 ... Building completed for Castle Hill, home of marine biologist and Harvard professor Alexander Agassiz

1884.... Rear Admiral Stephen B. Luce founds the Naval War College

1908 ... Cardines Field—then called Basin Field—baseball stadium opens, destined to host both legends and amateur ballers

1930 ... America's Cup held in Newport for the first time

1954 ... First Newport Jazz Festival. Newport Folk begins a few years later, in 1959.

1983.... *Liberty* loses to *Australia II* in the final America's Cup yacht race hosted in Newport

1995 ... ESPN Extreme Games [later X Games] debuts with skateboarding events at Fort Adams State Park

2012 ... Hurricane Sandy washes away a large portion of the Cliff Walk

ABOUT TOWN

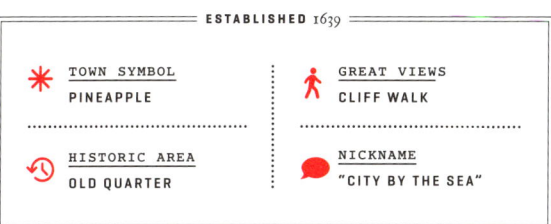

=== ESTABLISHED 1639 ===

TOWN SYMBOL
PINEAPPLE

HISTORIC AREA
OLD QUARTER

GREAT VIEWS
CLIFF WALK

NICKNAME
"CITY BY THE SEA"

CIVIC LIFE

FAMED MAYOR
Harry Winthrop
2012-14 and 2016-18

HISTORIC SOCIAL CLUB
Newport Casino
194 Bellevue Ave

UNIVERSITY
Salve Regina
Established 1947

LARGEST EMPLOYER
The U.S. Navy
9,000 personnel

SERVICES

TAILOR
Mery's Tailor Shop
10 Marlborough St

GADGET REPAIR
Cove Electronics
40 Broadway

BARBER
Hair Apparent
424 Thames St

VENETIAN PLASTER
Flavio Bragaloni
@flaviobragaloni

NAVIGATION

From May through October, this compact city by the sea becomes even easier to explore than usual thanks to the Jamestown Newport Ferry. This low-key way to cross town has five hop-on, hop-off stops: Jamestown, Rose Island Lighthouse, Fort Adams, Ann Street Pier and Perrotti Park. Ticket options include one-way or round-trip, plus a special evening rate after 4 p.m. Bonus: All vessels come equipped with a bar and refreshments.

SELECTED CONTENT

016–017　*Food & Drink*

　　　　　BAKERY
　　　　　LOBSTER ROLL
　　　　　COLONIAL TAVERN
　　　　　CLAM CHOWDER

018　　　*Shopping*

　　　　　BOOKS
　　　　　VINTAGE
　　　　　FLOWERS
　　　　　SUITING

019　　　*Action*

　　　　　NATURE WALK
　　　　　CRUISE
　　　　　OYSTER FARM
　　　　　LOCAL PERFORMANCE

020　　　*Arts & Culture*

　　　　　MANSION TOURS
　　　　　CINEMA
　　　　　DANCE COMPANY
　　　　　TOPIARY

021　　　*Experts*

　　　　　BLACK HISTORY
　　　　　STONE CARVING
　　　　　SURFING
　　　　　PUMP OUT

　　　　　MORE THAN 70 PICKS ⤶

BESTS

A curated list of town favorites—classic and new—from bars and restaurants to shops and experiences, plus a handful of can't-miss experts

BESTS

FOOD & DRINK

STEAKHOUSE
22 Bowen's
*22 Bowen's Wharf
Newport*
À la carte steak, seafood and more. Nautical-themed dining room.
....

FRENCH BAKERY
Le Bec Sucré
*696 Aquidneck Ave
Middletown*
Viennoiseries and baguettes from Parisian pastry chef Belinda Quinn.
....

COFFEE
The Nitro Bar
*2 Pond Ave
Newport*
Nitro cold brew, specialty lattes, breakfast bites. Community vibes at two brick-and-mortar locations.

OYSTERS
Midtown Oyster Bar
*345 Thames St
Newport*
Raw bar, seafood towers and daily catch. First floor: tavern; second floor: Burgee Bar.
....

BEACH TREAT
Del's Lemonade
All over
A summer sacrament. Frozen lemonade, frozen watermelon or half and half. No straws.
....

LOBSTER ROLL
Newport Lobster Shack
*150 Long Wharf
Newport*
Fresh-picked lobster, mayo and celery on a toasted bun. Side of chips or chowder.

DIVE
The Fastnet Pub
*1 Broadway
Newport*
Traditional Irish pub with sports bar mojo and live music.
....

RAMEN
Yagi Noodles
*20 Long Wharf Mall
Newport*
Japanese- and Chinese-inspired ramen. You're drinking boba or BYOB.
....

COLONIAL TAVERN
White Horse Tavern
*26 Marlborough St
Newport*
America's oldest operating restaurant, since 1673. Burnished colonial walls, classic New England-y menu. Scotch egg.

DINER
Franklin Spa
229 Spring St
Newport
Mom 'n' pop, hearty breakfast and lunch classics. Cash only.
....

CLAM CHOWDER
The Black Pearl
30 Bannister's Wharf
Newport
Enjoy a cup of famed chowder with wharfside views.
....

ICE CREAM
Clementine's
62 Wave Ave
Middletown
Chocolate coconut almond. Black raspberry chip. Clementine sorbet.
....

MEXICAN
Perro Salado
19 Charles St
Newport
Legit mole and tacos in a historic house.
....

ROOFTOP BAR
Crow's Nest
254 Thames St
Newport
Upstairs at Benjamin's. Take in the harbor views with a beer in hand.

JAMAICAN
Humming Bird
104 Broadway
Newport
Jerk chicken, oxtail, red bean stew.
....

PRIX FIXE
The Dining Room at Castle Hill Inn
590 Ocean Ave
Newport
Six courses of farm-to-table bounty.
....

APERITIVI
Giusto
4 Commercial Wharf
Newport
Freestyle Italian plus a biodynamic and natural wine list.
....

HOT DOGS
Wally's Wieners
464 Thames St
Newport
Toppings galore. Take The Wally Challenge if you're feeling frisky.
....

BLIND TASTING MENU
Cara
117 Memorial Blvd
Newport
Contemporary, Euro-inspired dishes. Private dining at The Chanler.

FANCY NIGHT
The SkyBar
24 Bannister's Wharf
Newport
New England fare in Clarke Cooke House. Jacket required.
....

NEW-WORLD MARKET
Leo's
162 Broadway
Newport
Homemade Latin American eats.
....

RED SAUCE JOINT
Mamma Luisa
673 Thames St
Newport
Bolognese, arrabiata, vongole: that's amore.
....

FARM-FOCUSED
TSK
509 Thames St
Newport
Local, seasonal ingredients. Spotlight on sustainability.
....

TAQUERIA
La Vecina
24 Washington Sq
Newport
James Beard nominee Mariana Gonzalez-Trasvina's homage to her Mexico City roots.

SHOPS

INDIE BOOKSTORE
Charter Books
8 Broadway
Newport
Mix of bestsellers, local authors and small-press gems.
....

GARDEN
Cottage & Garden
9 Bridge St
Newport
A trove of countryside-estate aesthetics.
....

TCHOTCHKES
Primavera
4 Bowen's Wharf
Newport
A range of wares and gifts with a distinctly local bent.
....

ARCHITECTURAL ANTIQUES
Aardvark Antiques
9 JT Connell Hwy
Newport
Life-size animal statues and a chandelier collection. Like walking through the looking glass.

VINTAGE
Folk
446 Thames St
Newport
Retro and recycled finds. Channeling the '70s, disco ball included.
....

UPCYCLED SAILS
Re-Sails
364 Thames St
Newport
A Newport original. Sporty bags and accessories made of recycled sailcloth.
....

OUTFITTER
Big Weather Gear
154 Thames St
Newport
The go-to retailer for water, wind or snow.
....

SUITING
Michael Hayes
204 Bellevue Ave
Newport
Synonymous with Newport style. Known for custom-tailoring services.

FINE BRITISH GARMENTS
Royal Male
104 Spring St
Newport
Old-world style hub and source for European panache.
....

DIVING GEAR
The Dive Shop
550 Thames St
Newport
Snorkeling kit and certification classes.
....

BLOOMS
Wild Season Florals
174 Green End Ave
Middletown
Stunning floral arrangements and an impressive gifts selection.
....

NEW ENGLAND LOOKS
Kiel James Patrick
3 Bowen's Wharf
Newport
Nautical-inspired knitwear and accessories. All jewelry handmade in Rhode Island.

ACTION

DANCING
Boom Boom Room
24 Bannister's Wharf
Newport
The late-night downstairs dancing spot, complete with mirrored DJ booth.

....

GOAT HIKES
Simmons Farm
1942 West Main Rd
Middletown
Stroll with your new caprine friends, exploring bucolic scenery.

....

SUNSET CRUISE
Rum Runner II
cruisenewport.com
Newport Harbor motor yacht tour. Cocktails included.

....

OYSTER FARM TOURS
Matunuck Oyster Farm
629 Succotash Rd
Wakefield
See shellfish in their briny aquacultural beds. Slurp oyster after oyster.

NATURE WALK
Norman Bird Sanctuary
583 3rd Beach Rd
Middletown
Hiking trails and bird sightings. Bring your binoculars.

....

STRAWBERRY PICKING
Sweet Berry Farm
915 Mitchell's Ln
Middletown
Pick-your-own fruit farm with market and cafe on site.

....

PERFORMANCE SPACE
Casino Theatre
10 Freebody St
Newport
An 1880s gem, restored as home to Salve Regina University theater, dance and music programs.

....

MOMENT OF ZEN
Sachuest Point
769 Sachuest Point Rd, Middletown
Wildlife refuge and stopover for migratory birds.

COMEDY
Rogue Island Comedy Fest
rogueislandcomedyfest.com
Semiannual [spring, fall], led by locals.

....

FLYING A KITE
Kitt Kites
481 Ocean Ave
Newport
Nylon kites for all skill levels.

....

GLASSBLOWING
Thames Glass
688 Thames St
Newport
Book an appointment to blow your own masterpiece.

....

SAILING RACE
New York Yacht Club Regatta
June
The nation's oldest.

....

MUSIC FESTIVALS
newportfolk.org
newportjazz.org
newportclassical.org
Iconic summertime sonic celebrations.

ARTS & CULTURE

MANSION TOURS

Preservation Society of Newport County
newportmansions.org
Official caretakers of Newport's crown architectural jewels.

....

FILM SERIES

newportFILM Outdoors
newportfilm.com
Weekly documentary showings under the summer stars.

....

HISTORIC CINEMA

The Jane Pickens Theater
49 Touro St Newport
The reel started spinning before there were talkies.

....

DANCE

Newport Contemporary Ballet
3 Charles St Newport
Transforming the dance experience for over 40 years.

JEWELRY

Lazuli Handcrafted
6 Deblois St Newport
Handmade from raw, recycled materials.

....

FLOWER SHOW

The Newport Flower Show
newportmansions.org
Horticultural town takeover.

....

ARTIST-OWNED GALLERY

Kristen Coates
152 Bellevue Ave Newport
Fine art meets refined homeware.

....

LIBRARY

Redwood Library & Athenaeum
50 Bellevue Ave Newport
America's first purpose-built library. Still lends books out of its original building.

CLASSIC CARS

Audrain Auto Museum
222 Bellevue Ave Newport
Rotating exhibits of old-school rides, far back as the 1800s.

....

TOPIARY

Green Animals Topiary Garden
380 Corys Ln Portsmouth
Seven acres of sculpted trees, gardens, walkways.

....

COLONIAL

Newport Restoration Foundation
newportrestoration.org
Guardians of the city's architecture. Three museums, more than 70 homes.

....

COMEDY

The Bit Players
bitplayers.net
High-energy, BYOB improv shows at the Firehouse Theater.

EXPERTS

OCEAN CONSERVATION
Clean Ocean Access Team
cleanoceanaccess.org
Local heroes known for protecting shoreline access. Beach clean-up hosts.

....

MASSAGE
Kenji Omori
kenjiomorilmt.com
The person to see for lasting deep-tissue relief. Therapeutic touch.

....

BLACK HISTORY
Keith Stokes
1696heritage.com
Nationally renowned Newport, illuminating early African and Jewish American history.

....

HELICOPTER TOURS
Jeff Codman
newporthelicoptertours.com
Bird's Eye View tour and charter founder, aviating since age 12.

LOCAL FOODWAYS
Rhode Island Red Food Tours
rhodeislandredfoodtours.com
Introducing the culinarily curious to local culture via edible specialties.

....

OYSTER FARMER
Perry Raso
rhodyoysters.com
Aquaculturist and educator got his start digging for littlenecks in Point Judith Pond.

....

FILM
Andrea van Beuren
@sustainablefilms
Founder and artistic director of newportFILM, now spearheading Sustainable Films.

....

PUMP OUT
John Hartnett
VHF Channel 9
Motorboat expert taking care of the harbor's dirty work.

STONE CARVING
Nicholas Benson
johnstevensshop.com
Third-generation carver and a MacArthur Fellow.

....

CONSERVATIONIST
Natasha Harrison
natashaharrison.com
Current head of the Newport Tree Conservancy, former head of the Norman Bird Sanctuary.

....

ANTIQUARIAN BOOKSELLER
Elizabeth Young
lizzyoungbookseller.com
Specializing in vintage tomes and publications with a gastronomic or societal bent.

....

SURFING
Island Surf & Sport
islandsports.com
New England's largest surf shop. Loyal to locals: in-person sales only.

SELECTED CONTENT

024 *Socialites of Note*
025 *Newport Folk Festival*
026 *Goddard & Townsend*
027 *Ida Lewis & John Lennon*
029 *League of American Wheelmen*
030 *Newport Mercury*
031 *God's Little Acre*
033 *The Kennedys*
034 *America's Cup*
035 *Newport Jazz Festival*
036 *Tennis & Croquet*
037 *Indigenous Place Names*
039 *Religion*
040 *Dylan Goes Electric*
043 *The Breakers*

ALMANAC

A deep dive into the cultural heritage of Newport through news clippings, timelines and other historical hearsay

SOCIALITES OF NOTE

ALVA BELMONT

Born in Mobile, Alabama, in 1853, Alva Belmont relocated with her family to New York City just before the Civil War. Once successful cotton brokers, their status fluctuated—until Alva married William K. Vanderbilt in 1875. She quickly became known for buildings she commissioned, from multiple Fifth Avenue dwellings in New York City to the Marble House mansion in Newport. She divorced Vanderbilt in 1895, marrying Oliver Hazard Perry Belmont a year later. After his death in 1908, Belmont took interest in philanthropy and politics; she staged a suffragist operetta, opened her Newport mansion to feminist rallies, and founded the Political Equality League. Allegedly, she loved to offer this advice: "Pray to God. She will help you."

CAROLINE ASTOR

Perhaps the ultimate socialite of her time. She came from undeniably old money, by way of Dutch aristocracy [New York's prominent Schermerhorns], and her fortune grew when she married William Astor, grandson of fur baron John Jacob Astor, in 1853. She was a leader of society from New York to Newport, even Paris, hosting balls, teas, receptions, late-night dinners and all manner of *fête* year-round. Naturally, Astor spent summers at her Newport home, Beechwood.

DORIS DUKE

Dubbed "the debutante who broke all the rules" by *The New York Times*, this tobacco heiress was born post-Gilded Age in 1912. However, her penchant for luxury and her sheer wealth [she inherited more than $50 million at the age of 12] mirrored the lives of her predecessors. She summered at her family's cottage, Rough Point, and married twice with little success. By the '50s, Duke was a philanthropist divorcée, dividing time among five homes, including the Newport mansion, a hillside manor in Beverly Hills and her art-filled estate in Hawai'i, Shangri La. She infamously killed her friend and art curator, Eduardo Tirella, when she ran him over with her car outside the gates of Rough Point on October 8, 1966; Tirella's death was declared an accident [circumstances were murky]. In 1968, Duke founded the Newport Restoration Foundation to revitalize celebrated estates.

THE NEWPORT FOLK FESTIVAL

1958 .....Long-running Boston jazz club Storyville begins Sunday folk-music nights

1959 .....Storyville owner [and Newport Jazz Fest founder] George Wein launches Folk Fest

.....Famed manager Albert Grossman books Pete Seeger, New Lost City Ramblers, Odetta

1960.....Expanded to three nights, emphasizing international folk traditions

1963 .....Friday night: Bill Monroe, Bob Dylan, Doc Watson, Joan Baez, Peter, Paul & Mary

.....Saturday night: Bessie Jones, John Lee Hooker, Judy Collins, Pete Seeger

.....Mississippi John Hurt plays Saturday blues workshop, Sunday evening main stage, reviving 1920s career

.....Baez and Student Nonviolent Coordinating Committee lead civil rights march, cementing festival rep for activism

1965 .....Folk purists outraged as Dylan "goes electric"

1969 .....Johnny Cash introduces a promising rookie: Kris Kristofferson

.....Songwriters Workshop features Joni Mitchell, James Taylor, Paul Geremia [not too shabby]

.....Taylor's debut set cut off after 15 minutes due to moon landing

1970.....Festival discontinued due to local controversies [Jazz Fest suspended the following year after crowd safety issues]

1985 .....Folk fest relaunch features Baez, Ramblin' Jack Elliott, Bonnie Raitt, Taj Mahal, etc.

1986.....15-year-old fiddle player Alison Krauss is a highlight, but attendance lags. UPI: "Newport Folk Draws Laid-Back Music Fans; Future Uncertain."

1990.....Michelle Shocked orchestrates V-J Day ["Hiroshima Day"] die-in

2002.....Bob Dylan returns—in wig and fake beard

2009 ....Jam session unites Pete Seeger and The Decemberists

2022......Joni Mitchell's regal return, backed by Brandi Carlisle, gets rapturous response

GODDARD AND TOWNSEND

"Doris Duke Pays Record Price of $102,000 for Goddard Piece"
Newport Mercury, May 28, 1971

Miss Doris Duke, president of the Newport Restoration Foundation, is the purchaser of the world's most expensive piece of furniture, high-placed sources in the New York art world disclosed today. The furniture, a Goddard Chippendale carved bonnet mahogany highboy, fetched a world's record price of $102,000 during spirited bidding Saturday at Parke-Bernet's Manhattan galleries. Foundation sources were unable to confirm the report that Miss Duke's foundation, which is restoring more than 60 Colonial homes in the area, made the purchase. … When the magic figure of $100,000 was reached, spectators gasped. A $2,000 raise in the bid by [art collector and gallerist] Malcolm Vallance closed the deal. … The Goddards and the Townsends were two families of cabinetmakers during the 17th and 18th centuries. The families intermarried and produced four generations of Newport craftsmen known worldwide for excellent craftsmanship in production of Queen Anne and Chippendale styles.

> *The Quaker Goddard-Townsend furniture dynasty was known for its carved scallop shells, ball-and-claw feet and block fronts. John Goddard, the most famous individual in the sprawling family tree, died a poor man in 1785, leaving his family wood scraps and debt. Two centuries later, in 1990, a single desk from his workbench sold for $12 million.*

NAVY BULLETIN

April 2023 — Naval Station Newport's Ney Hall Galley was named the best East Coast General Mess for Fiscal Year 2023. The galley, named for Capt. Edward F. Ney, and for whom the annual awards are named, was among seven Navy recipients … recognized for excellence in food service. "Naval Station Newport is a Navy center of excellence," said Janet Lamb, food services officer at the galley and a retired Navy supply corps officer. "Nothing has a more positive impact on the personnel we serve than the top-notch meals we turn out. Meeting this objective, in spite of some of the challenges we face, is the daily reward our team gets."

IDA LEWIS

"THE GUARDIAN ANGEL OF NEWPORT HARBOR"
New-York Daily Tribune
April 12, 1869

Fast paralyzing with cold and almost bereft of hope the two soldiers saw no choice left but to clasp each other in a last embrace, and sink to a mutual grave—when suddenly, out from Lime Rock, half a mile away, shot a little boat, driven by rapid strokes and sure, straight over the bounding waves toward the drowning men. Hope kindled in their breasts again, but faded when they saw in the boat only a slender youth, and a still slenderer woman plying the oars. On it swiftly came, however, and the boy was almost reaching over the side to grasp the nearest soldier, when his quick-witted sister, crying, "Stop, Hosey! We shall be capsized that way!" turned the boat with a well-timed stroke, backed it up, one man was drawn safely in over the stern, another backward pull, another lift, and then next moment the craft, with its freight of rescued lives, was scudding swiftly through the spray back to the Rock again.

While it was only one of her many rescues, this exploit earned Idawalley Zoradia Lewis national renown. She was dubbed "The Bravest Woman in America." Today, the lighthouse she kept for 54 years bears her name and is cared for by the Ida Lewis Yacht Club.

JOHN LENNON

A remarkable maritime episode in the life of a Beatle.

On June 4, 1980, the 43-foot sloop *Megan Jaye* left Newport Harbor with a particularly famous passenger: John Lennon. During its 650-mile trip to Bermuda, the boat hit a nasty storm, and after days of exhaustion, the crew recruited novice sailor Lennon to helm it. For six overnight hours, he fought the rain and waves alone. The next morning, the crew found him a man transformed. Upon disembarking, he signed the passenger log: "Dear Megan, there's no place like nowhere."

ALMANAC

LEAGUE OF AMERICAN WHEELMEN

"BICYCLE RIDERS AT NEWPORT"
The New York Times, May 30, 1880

Over 100 bicycle riders have reached Newport in readiness for the "meet" to-morrow. Twenty-nine clubs from Washington, Baltimore, Philadelphia, Chicago, Trenton, New-York, Saratoga, Brooklyn, Hartford, New-Haven, Worcester, Providence, Boston, and elsewhere are represented. A meeting was held at the Aquidneck House to-day, E.C. Pratt, of Boston, presiding. J. Frank Burrill, of New-York, acted as Secretary. It was voted that the organization to be formed to-morrow shall be called the "League of American Wheelmen." The following committee was appointed to draft a constitution: C.E. Pratt, of Boston; J. Frank Burrill and C.K. Monroe, New-York; S.F. Clark, Baltimore; S.A. Marsden, New-Haven, and J.M. Fairfield, Chicago. The proceedings to-morrow will comprise a meeting of the Captains at 9 o'clock, convention at the Rink at 10, parade at 1:30, and a banquet at 5:30.

> *The "Wheelmen" may seem antique in name, but we have them in large part to thank for today's paved roads. Yesteryear's thoroughfares were clogged with wagons, trolleys, sewage and trash. As elites took to biking—"penny farthing" cycles were expensive—they began to lobby for better conditions, and the LAW was formed. Today, the League of American Bicyclists—same group, newer name—still advocates for improved riding conditions and shared roads with their mission: "To create a Bicycle Friendly America for everyone."*

From "Wheelman's Song"
by Will Carleton, 1884

Good-morning, fellow-wheelmen,—here's a warm fraternal hand,
As, with a rush of victory, we sweep across the land! ...
We claim a great utility that daily must increase;
We claim from inactivity a sensible release;
A constant mental, physical, and moral help we feel,
That bids us turn enthusiasts, and cry, "God bless the wheel!"

ALMANAC

NEWPORT MERCURY

Headlines from "The Oldest Paper in America."

OCTOBER 1, 1770
"Undaunted by TYRANTS,—We'll DIE or Be FREE"

JANUARY 19, 1822
"More Pirates Taken"

AUGUST 25, 1883
"The Yacht *Ideal* a Total Wreck"

JANUARY 3, 1920
"Death Wave Due to Fake Whiskey"

APRIL 4, 1930
"Alvah H. Sanborn Dies of Acute Indigestion"

DECEMBER 12, 1941
"Odd Fellows Hold Indoor Clambake"

APRIL 6, 1951
"State, Middletown Police Seize Pinball Machine"

JULY 25, 1969
"Diggers Ignore Quahaug Limit"

AUGUST 7, 1970
"Eight Colorful Balloons Float Over Old Mansion"

DECEMBER 16, 1977
"Music Was Made for Waltzing but No Room to Dance Existed"

JANUARY 16, 2018
"'Grumpy Guy Doing Magic in a Dragon Costume'"

Founded in 1758 by Ann Smith Franklin [yes, relation to Ben], the Newport Mercury *ceased publication in 2018.*

GOD'S LITTLE ACRE

Newport was one of the most active colonial seaports, particularly when it came to the trade of rum, wax candles and slaves. Ships brought abducted people here, primarily from West Africa; over time, a community of free people of color coalesced in Newport. Located on Farewell Street, the cemetery known as "God's Little Acre" is said to be the nation's earliest and largest surviving collection of grave markers of enslaved and free Africans and African Americans.

"Today, in our Common Burying Ground along Farewell Street in the northwest corner, as early as 1705, we have initially enslaved and later free Africans. We have the largest concentration of free and enslaved African burials—the existing stones as they originally were set and carved and marked—not in the American South, not in the West Indies, not in Boston, not New York, but right here in Newport. By the mid part of the 19th century, the African American community would lovingly call it 'God's Little Acre.' God's Little Acre today is recognized not only for its importance of having so many markers, but it's finally being recognized for the fact that it also includes markers with etchings that begin to tell the story of where Africans originated from, their lives and eventual deaths. They're telling a story in stone that's not about chattel property. It's not about slaves and beasts of the field. It's men, women and children who persevered, who survived and left the legacy of this burial ground here in Newport. As a young boy, my grandmother would say repeatedly, 'Slavery is how we got here, but it tells you little about who we are as people.' The stories of stone that I'm presenting you today are not the stories of chattel property. They're the stories of the people." —*Keith Stokes, TEDxNewport, 2019*

BURIAL MARKERS

In Memory of Prince
Son of Prince & Bynah Amy
Died 4 May 1778
Age 4 Years 4 Months

....

Sacred in the memory of Rosanna
widow of Simeon Taylor
who died May 18, 1847 in the 76th year

ALMANAC

REFLECTIONS ON NEWPORT

ALEXIS DE TOCQUEVILLE *From a letter to his mother,* 1831
"It's a collection of small houses, the size of chicken coops, distinguished by a cleanness that is a pleasure to see and that we have no conception of in France."

OSCAR WILDE *From a letter to Charles Eliot Norton,* 1882
"This little island where idleness ranks among the virtues."

ALVA VANDERBILT BELMONT 1895-1909
"Summer-publicity center of the nation."

MARK TWAIN *From* The Autobiography of Mark Twain, 1907
"Newport, Rhode Island, that breeding place—that stud farm, so to speak—of aristocracy; aristocracy of the American type."

HENRY ADAMS *From* The Education of Henry Adams, 1907
"Newport was charming, but it asked for no education and it gave none."

KURT VONNEGUT *From* The Sirens of Titan, 1959
"The town was Newport, Rhode Island, U.S.A., Earth, Solar System, Milky Way."

DWIGHT D. EISENHOWER *From remarks upon the dedication of Eisenhower Park,* 1960
"I suspect that future presidents will learn something about this place and the fun we have had here, and possibly they will even come to try it themselves. And if they do, they will repeat."

JOHN F. KENNEDY *From remarks at America's Cup dinner,* 1962
"I know that all of us take the greatest pleasure in being here, first of all because … we are all joined by a common interest, a common devotion and love for the sea."

JAY LENO *As told to* Architectural Digest, 2019
"Newport is ocean all around. Newport is also one of those places that has that New England attitude—it's funnier than any place in America. That suspicious 'What brings you here?'"

SUMMER WHITE HOUSE

Newport Daily News
June 30, 1961

President and Mrs. Kennedy plan to spend most of their vacation in Newport after Congress adjourns, probably late in August, it became known today. The Summer White House will be at "Hammersmith Farm," the Harrison Avenue estate of Mrs. Kennedy's step-father and mother, Mr. and Mrs. Hugh D. Auchincloss. According to their present plans, the Kennedys and their two children will be at "Hammersmith Farm" most of each week. They will go to the Kennedy summer home in Hyannis Port, Mass., weekends. … T. Robert Primmerman, local manager of the New England Telephone Co., said today no word had been received by him about the president coming to Newport. The company would be required to install the extensive communications systems required. The one set up for President Eisenhower has been dismantled and an entire new system would have to be set up, Primmerman said.

ALEXANDER AGASSIZ

The son of a Swiss scientist changed the landscape of marine biology, and built a Newport institution.

"Unless he is in some far away, little known quarter of the globe, studying the roots of the coral islands or nosing about after such other secrets of nature as are to be found only at the bottom of the ocean, a certain rather broad, rather short, rather athletic-looking man may be seen on almost every working morning between the first of October and the first of June striding briskly and with a military air to the entrance of one of the dignified buildings connected with Harvard University. … Strictly speaking, Alexander Agassiz has been a scientist all his life. He was born to be one: his childhood in Switzerland, his boyhood in Cambridge, his years in college and at Lawrence Scientific School, his coast survey work in California and his place as assistant in zoology at Harvard were all passed in a scientific atmosphere."
—The Courier-Journal, *Louisville, Kentucky, December 24,* 1905

AMERICA'S CUP

"*Shamrock V* Goes Over Part of Course in Snappy Breeze"
Newport Mercury
September 5, 1930

The green sloop of Sir Thomas Lipton, which will wage a spirited battle with the *Enterprise* in the international races next month, received her first real taste of race conditions in American waters Friday, when she went over part of the course during a snappy breeze and choppy waters. Under these conditions the challenger from the British Isles made an impressive showing, and those who witnessed the performance were of the opinion that the races between the challenger and defender will present keener competition than the last set, when the *Resolute* defeated the *Shamrock IV*. The *Shamrock V* was sweeping over the waters like a ghost ship when she made off shore. She turned toward Narragansett, where those who were manoeuvering her could test the air currents in that vicinity, and then tacked toward the southeast. Reaching Block Island waters under a ballooner, she turned and made the run home under a spinnaker.

> *America's Cup, the oldest still-extant international sporting competition, has been contested just 37 times since 1851. Twelve of those installments took place in Newport's waters, as the New York Yacht Club repeatedly defeated challengers from abroad. [Sir Thomas Lipton, tea magnate, lost five consecutive attempts to win the cup.] In 1983, an Australian boat defeated American yachtsman Dennis Conner—and the race has never since returned to Newport.*

CUP-WINNING BOATS AT NEWPORT

Enterprise .... USA, 1930
Rainbow .... USA, 1934
Ranger .... USA, 1937
Columbia .... USA, 1958
Weatherly .... USA, 1962
Constellation .... USA, 1964
Intrepid .... USA, 1970
Courageous ...... USA, 1974 & 1977
Freedom .... USA, 1980
Australia II ..... AUSTRALIA, 1983

NEWPORT JAZZ FESTIVAL

Selected live albums.

ELLINGTON AT NEWPORT 1956
Landmark double set. Sax player Paul Gonsalves' all-out marathon solo brings down the house.

TOSHIKO AND LEON SASH AT NEWPORT 1957
Pianist Toshiko Akiyoshi, noted for innovation as a bandleader, pairs up with accordionist Sash.

AFTER THE RIOT AT NEWPORT 1960
The Nashville All-Stars—Chet Atkins and friends—jam outside a nearby mansion after crowd disturbances cancel their festival set.

BITCHES BREW LIVE *recorded* 1969; *released* 2011
Miles Davis goes electric. Three intense Newport cuts join a 1970 Isle of Wight set.

THE LAST SET AT NEWPORT 1971
Dave Brubeck lays it down just before a riot [a different riot] interrupts proceedings, causing long fest hiatus from Newport.

COUNT BASIE AT NEWPORT 1957
Possibly the big-band genre's ultimate hour. John Hammond's debonair intro is a treat in itself.

ELLA FITZGERALD AND BILLIE HOLIDAY AT NEWPORT 1958
One power-packed side from each. Rough-around-the-edges recording, but all the better for it.

HERBIE MANN AT NEWPORT 1963
A warm breeze from the flute player, heavy on Brazilian bossa nova classics. Cocktail party must-have.

RAY CHARLES AT NEWPORT 1958
A big groove from Ray, as one might expect. Six-minute rave on "I've Got A Woman."

ORIGINAL 9

On September 23, 1970, the Original 9—Billie Jean King, Rosie Casals, Nancy Richey, Kristy Pigeon, Valerie Ziegenfuss, Peaches Bartkowicz, Kerry Melville Reid, Judy Tegart Dalton and Julie Heldman—signed with promoter and World Tennis Magazine *founder Gladys Heldman to create the first professional women's tennis tournament. In 2021, King offered these remarks in Newport, upon the 9's induction to the Tennis Hall of Fame.*

"It's an honor and privilege to stand with these women and make history once again. … We are the Original Nine: Valerie Ziegenfuss, Kristy Pigeon, Julie Heldman, Peaches Bartkowicz, Kerry Melville Reid—a special thanks to Rosie Casals for believing the Original Nine belong in the International Tennis Hall of Fame—and the two of us who couldn't be here tonight. The nine of us, along with our fearless leader Gladys Heldman, had one vision for the future of women's tennis. We wanted any girl in the world, if she was good enough, to have a place to compete, to be recognized for her accomplishments, not only her looks. And most importantly, to be able to make a living playing professional tennis. And today's women's professional tennis players on the WTA Tour are living our dream. Women's tennis is the leader in women's sports."

CROQUET

No man invented whist or chess, and croquet like them seems to have been evolved by some process of nature, as a crystal forms or a flower grows—perfect, in accordance with eternal laws. There is in all these games a certain theory which furnishes interpretations for all cases that arise in actual play. The mimic battles have a unity. … If the rules are indefinite or contradictory the game loses its distinctive character. If the rules are accurate and rigidly enforced, croquet is a game of the highest interest. I am informed by a scientific billiard player that though croquet is inferior in affording opportunities for delicate manipulation … it far exceeds that elegant game in the field it opens for the exercise of the higher qualities of combination and foresight.
—*Croquet: As Played by the Newport Croquet Club*, 1865

INDIGENOUS PLACE NAMES

AQUIDNECK ISLAND Derived from the Narragansett word *aquidnet* [which is thought to mean "at the island"], this was Rhode Island's original name and the longstanding term for Newport's geographic home.

NARRAGANSETT BAY Named for Rhode Island's largest tribe, which had settled much of the land surrounding the bay before colonization. New England's largest estuary and Newport's life source.

MIANTONOMI MEMORIAL PARK Named for the distinguished Narragansett chief, this park marks Newport's highest point. It was a strategic stronghold for the tribe and, after 1637, the British.

CONANICUT ISLAND Uncle of Miantonomi and chief of the Narragansett when the Pilgrims landed at Plymouth, the island's namesake kept a royal residence here, visible from Newport's western coast.

SACHUEST POINT Meaning "Little Hill at the Outlet." Today, it's a national wildlife refuge home to piping plovers, saltmarsh sparrows and snowy owls.

> *The Narragansett tribe endured and maintains a strong presence in Rhode Island, with traditional gatherings taking place at the Four Winds Community Center in Charlestown. The Tomaquag Indian Museum, located in Exeter, won the 2016 National Medal for Museum and Library Service and is the state's only museum dedicated to and run by Indigenous people.*

WILLIAM TROST RICHARDS

This painter, whose life stretched a great arc from 1833 to 1905, dedicated his eye to Newport's surf, land and light. His style connects to the famed Hudson Valley school and the romance of the natural that suffused American painting at large in the era when he lived and practiced. But in works like *From Paradise to Purgatory, Newport* [Metropolitan Museum, New York] and *Newport Coast* [Philadelphia Museum of Art], he marks himself as a visual bard of this place, above all.

BOAT GLOSSARY

What's what in Newport Harbor, as defined by dictionaries and described by sea dogs.

KAYAK Narrow craft, pointed at both ends and closed over the top. In July, spotted paddling out to Fort Adams to catch Folk Fest from the water.

DINGHY A smaller boat; can be sail or power, hard or inflatable. The craft of choice for young locals heading to secret swimming holes.

FERRY Boat of any size that moves people from one point of shore to another point of shore, whether across town, to other islands, or up to Providence.

SLOOP Single-masted sailboat with a mainsail and a forward jib. May race in groups across the harbor on summer nights.

SCHOONER A sailboat with at least two masts, where the frontmost one is smaller. Visitors hop aboard the *Madeline* or the *Adirondack II* for harbor cruises.

FISHING TRAWLER Commercial vessel built to pull fishing nets through the water. Not to be confused with lobster boats: equally hefty, salty craft used for pulling up lobster pots.

12-METER A particular type of racing sailboat that allows for experimentation with design while remaining within its class. Synonymous with Newport's America's Cup glory days.

CRUISER "Midsize" recreational powerboat, typically with living accommodations. Parked en masse along Newport's downtown docks throughout the summer months.

SUPERYACHT Also known as a "megayacht," these pleasure cruisers can measure upward of 130 feet. Walk to the middle of the Goat Island bridge and you're likely to spot some of the largest in the world.

TALL SHIP Many kinds of large sailing boats with multiple masts, all indeed very tall. Rhode Island's historic SSV *Oliver Hazard Perry* floats majestically at Fort Adams and is used as an instructional vessel.

RELIGION

1638..... Puritan Anne Hutchinson, driven out of Boston for progressive beliefs, settles with followers in the Pocasset area of Rhode Island
1639..... William Coddington and Nicholas Easton split off from Pocasset group, establish town of Newport
1644..... First Baptist church in Newport founded by John Clarke
1651..... Seventh Day Baptists separate from Clarke's church
1657..... The Society of Friends [a.k.a. Quakers] arrives on ship *Woodhouse*
1658..... First Jews arrive in Newport, escaping Inquisition in Brazil
1698..... Trinity Church constructed, serving Anglicans
1699..... Great Friends Meeting House: today, R.I.'s oldest house of worship
1730..... Seventh Day Baptist Meeting House constructed
1694..... Second wave of Jews comes to Newport via Curaçao
1759 .... Construction begins on Touro Synagogue
1763 .... Touro completed, now oldest synagogue in U.S.
1828..... Newport's first Catholic church, amid significant Irish immigration

Letter from George Washington to the Hebrew Congregation of Newport, 1790

"If we have wisdom to make the best use of the advantages with which we are now favored, we cannot fail, under the just administration of a good government, to become a great and happy people. The citizens of the United States of America have a right to applaud themselves for having given to mankind examples of an enlarged and liberal policy—a policy worthy of imitation. All possess alike liberty of conscience and immunities of citizenship. It is now no more that toleration is spoken of as if it were the indulgence of one class of people that another enjoyed the exercise of their inherent natural rights, for, happily, the Government of the United States, which gives to bigotry no sanction, to persecution no assistance, requires only that they who live under its protection should demean themselves as good citizens in giving it on all occasions their effectual support."

While Rhode Island was the first English colony with religious freedom written into its royal charter, Indigenous and enslaved people did not enjoy those liberties.

DYLAN GOES ELECTRIC

The Broadside
Notes from a Variant Stanza Collector, by Ed Freeman
Volume IV, Number 13
August 18, 1965

Newport, Sunday night: there are probably as many different ideas as to what happened, and why, as there are people who saw it happen; following is my version of what may be a momentous occasion in folk music.

Bob Dylan comes on stage, electric guitar in hand and accompanied by the entire Paul Butterfield R&B band. He does three numbers including "Maggie's Farm" and "Like a Rolling Stone" [they all sounded more or less the same]; audience response at the end of the first is fairly good; after the second, only fair. Dylan walks off stage at the end of his third number, looking rather disgusted. Peter Yarrow tries to convince the audience that he had only been allotted time for three songs; somebody else said it was because he was sick or because he couldn't get together with Butterfield's band, but the real reason was rather obvious: he left the stage because he was being booed by a large segment of the audience. It seems that there are some people who don't like electrified, amplified, reverberated, echo-chambered, rock 'n' rolled Bob Dylan.

Dylan comes back on stage after a lot of coaxing, encouragement and bloody screams from the audience; but the second time around, he has an acoustic guitar with him, and he does two of his more folk-oriented obscurities, including "Tambourine Man," an obvious crowd-appeaser.

The importance of the event, however, lies not in what the crowd did or didn't like, but in the fact that they actually had enough taste and self-determination to have an opinion, that they could scream all week-end for their hero and then boo him for doing something they thought was bad. ... It is heartening to know that the masses [pardon me, the Great American Majority] has any taste at all, knows the difference between rock 'n' roll and folk music, and prefers to hear the latter at a folk festival.

Bob Dylan's set at the '65 Newport Folk Festival became one of pop music's most mythologized incidents. Controversy over crowd reaction persists. The classic D.A. Pennebaker documentary Don't Look Back *chronicles fallout from the stylistic shift.*

NEWPORT SOCIETY NOTES

Personal and General Gossip of the Rhode Island Resort.
The New York Times, Summer 1898

Aug. 2. — Count Deym of London is the guest of Mr. Lorillard Spencer.

J. Barton Willing of Philadelphia has arrived for the Summer.

The Saturday evening hop at the Ocean House was largely attended.

Many cards of welcome were left at The Breakers Saturday for Mr. and Mrs. Cornelius Vanderbilt.

The annual open tournament of the Newport Golf Club, which began today, will continue until Sept. 3. Prince Victor Emanuel has offered a cup for a golf match.

Aug. 16. — Mrs. I. Townsend Burden entertained at dinner this evening at Fairlawn, the guests being Mrs. Henry Clews, Mr. and Mrs. Harry Payne Whitney, Mr. Paul D'Hauteville, Miss Willing … Mr. and Mrs. Prescott Lawrence, Mr. and Mrs. George Henry Warren … Mr. R.A. Chanler, Miss Brice and Mr. Joostens of the Belgium Legation.

Mrs. John Clinton Gray gave a moonlight picnic at Gooseberry Island last evening in honor of her daughter, Miss Gray, who was recently formally introduced to society. The party of young people was chaperoned by Mrs. Gray and Miss Wolfe.

There is a report current that the cottagers are contemplating having Sousa's Band here for an entertainment shortly on the idea of a peace carnival.

The polo players and their ponies arrived from Narragansett Pier yesterday for to-morrow's match.

Mrs. Cornelius Vanderbilt will give a large dinner dance at the Breakers on Thursday.

Sept. 10. — All large dinner parties are now considered anything but complete without music. Music for the cottagers has become a necessity apparently, for one may hear reports almost daily that it would not be at all surprising when next season opens here to learn that orchestras had been brought to Newport by cottagers for their exclusive use, for small dances have been held most frequently after dinner parties.

Rumor has it that the Executive Committee of Spouting Rock Beach has decided to reduce the cost of bathhouse rentals next Summer.

GOLF

Newport Golf Club was home to the first-ever U.S. Open Championship, in 1895. A young Englishman named Horace Rawlins won $150. Today, the tournament winner takes home more than $3 million.

"NEW CLUBS BEING FORMED AND LINKS LAID OUT"
The Sun, June 16, 1895

Golf is swinging upward. Sports have their rise and fall, for there is a seesaw in recreations as well as in the serious affairs of life, and the "Royal and Ancient" game is now going up in public favor. Although the growth is fast, there is nothing of the "boom" about it. The present rush to form golf clubs, buy or lease land, or lay out links has a firm foundation. Ardent golfers transplanted as a rule from Scotland or England, have for years been doing missionary work at places far apart—Chicago, Boston, Denver, and New York—and preparing the way for the game. The acorns planted by the golfing pioneers have produced mighty oaks; in "booms" the tree is shown before the seed is in the ground.

THE BREAKERS

Newport Daily News, September 4, 1895

The social event last night was the gathering at "The Breakers" of about two hundred persons, upon invitation of Mr. and Mrs. Cornelius Vanderbilt, who provided for the evening's entertainment private theatricals, the play being "A Game of Romps." This is a bright comedy, giving the participants an opportunity to show to good advantage, and some of them, especially Mr. Cushing, proved that they have much ability. All acquitted themselves with credit. The women were presented with baskets of flowers festooned with bright silk ribbons. A dressing room was improvised on the stone terrace connected with the room. A stage was built in the large bow window of the drawing room, and a more cosy, picturesque scene would be difficult to imagine. The room is furnished in white and gold, in the Italian style. The "stage" curtains, which reached from the floor to the ceiling, were of rich maroon brocade, the whole being lighted by a massive gilt chandelier of many lights.

INCLUDED

046-048 **THE GILDED AGE**
The high society of bygone times left an indelible stamp on Newport. Explore mansions, art, design and legacy.

049-051 **BY THE SEA**
The meeting place of land and saltwater defines Newport. Look out on the ocean, or jump in it.

052-054 **SEAFOOD**
All that water brings forth great bounty. Feast on local oysters, lobsters and the one and only Bag of Donuts.

055-057 **OLD SPORT**
From tennis to golf to polo to sailing, Newport helped invent American sporting culture.

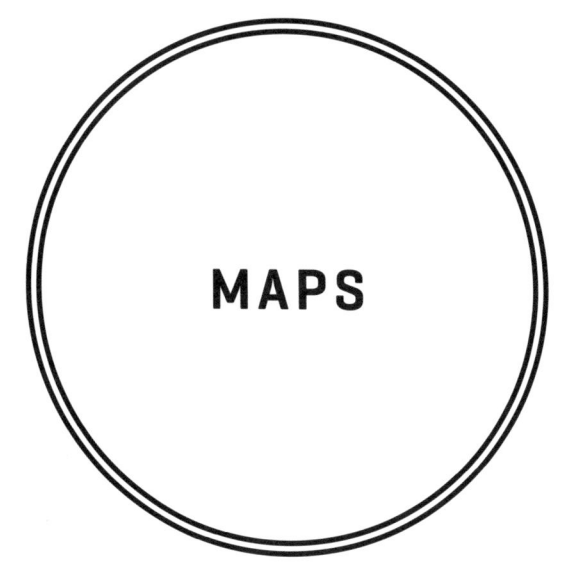

MAPS

Pictorial journeys through unique Newport culture,
commerce and landscape by illustrator
Andrew Desforges. Not to scale.

The Gilded Age

THE GILDED AGE

As America's wealthiest families flocked here in the late 19th century, the summer resort became a bastion of glamorous living and stunning architecture.

THE ELMS
Summer residence of coal-industry magnate Edward Julius Berwind, designed by Philadelphia architect Horace Trumbauer in the style of a mid-18th-century French chateau. 367 *Bellevue Ave*

THE BREAKERS
A glowing symbol of the Vanderbilt family's wealth, this so-called "cottage" features 70 rooms. Architect Richard Morris Hunt channeled Italy for its Renaissance Revival style. 44 *Ochre Point Ave*

KINGSCOTE
Landmark of Gothic Revival style built in 1839 by Richard Upjohn. Considered the first of the mansions in Newport's "cottage boom." 253 *Bellevue Ave*

CHINESE TEA HOUSE
Once a gathering place for Alva Vanderbilt's suffrage rallies, this Song dynasty-inspired building perches on a cliffside next to Marble House, another Vanderbilt mansion. Enjoy tea and brunch, $55 per person. 596 *Bellevue Ave*

THE DRAWING ROOM
This antique shop houses Gilded Age antiques galore. Pottery, textiles and glassware are among their specialties. 152 *Spring St*

THE BLUE GARDEN
A monochromatic garden landscaped by Frederick Law Olmsted Jr. at the tail end of the Gilded Age. Dotted with pergolas, pools and cerulean-hued plants. 32 *Washington St*

MARBLE HOUSE
The ruby-hued bedroom that once belonged to Consuelo Vanderbilt in this Bellevue Ave mansion serves as the fictional sleeping quarters for railroad tycoon George Russell in HBO's *The Gilded Age*.

RIDING COACH *The quaint pursuit of coach driving for sport resurfaces every three years in Newport during* A Weekend of Coaching. *Watch horse-drawn carriages parade around the mansions, next in August* 2024.

BY THE SEA

Nearly every Newport sight line ends with a water view, so even those who stick to land can feel like they earned their sea legs.

OCEAN DRIVE
Windows down: that's the only way to experience this 10-mile road that winds along stretches of beach, surveying rolling waves and historic mansions. *Coggeshall and Ocean avenues to Thames Street and Wellington Avenue*

EASTON'S BEACH
Known to locals simply as "First," this near-mile stretch of beach is Newport's longest, and it's where the city officially meets the sea. *175 Memorial Blvd*

SAFE HARBOR NEWPORT SHIPYARD
The working marina and shipyard where Newport's biggest yachts head for a tune-up. Never short on jaw-dropping vessels. *1 Washington St*

ROSE ISLAND LIGHTHOUSE
Accessible only by boat, Rose Island rents out its historic lighthouse. Experience 19th-century keepers' life. *Rose Island*

GOAT ISLAND
Here's some grim nautical history for fans of such content: In July, 1723, Newport authorities hanged 26 buccaneers here. [The port had previously been considered somewhat pirate-friendly.] The lore still looms large, as does that of an early rebellion's boat burning and, allegedly, Captain Cook's HMS *Endeavour*, sunken off shore. *Goat Island*

BANNISTER'S WHARF
Historically, Bannister's was one of two neighboring wharfs where goods and sailors came ashore. Today, it remains the heart of Newport Harbor and the launch point for several boat tours. *1 Bannister's Wharf*

REJECTS BEACH
A local fave: A sandy stretch where Newporters swim and sun themselves in defiance of the neighboring private beach club. Marks the far end of the Cliff Walk. *Bellevue and Coggeshall avenues*

SWIMMING HOLES *Keep tabs on the weekly water-monitoring reports from* Clean Ocean Access *for the clearest, safest spots to take a dip on any given day.*

MAPS

SEAFOOD

Newport specializes in only the freshest. From quahogs to calamari, this town's fishermen take the catch very seriously.

NEWPORT LOBSTER SHACK

No-frills access to the freshest crustaceans in town. Don't let the parking-lot locale fool you. This stuff is legit. *150 Long Wharf*

FLO'S CLAM SHACK

Clams, clams and more clams, any way you want 'em, since 1936. Founded in Flo's very own backyard chicken coop, now situated in a hurricane-proof beach cottage. *4 Wave Ave, Middletown*

BENJAMIN'S

Belly up to the raw bar for myriad offerings from the sea. Splurge on the Mother Shucker Platter, or tuck into a shrimp cocktail. *254 Thames St*

THE BLACK PEARL

Settle in at this atmosphere-rich tavern, where sailboats bob just outside. Grab a cup of clam chowder so good, they also sell it by the can. *30 Bannister's Wharf*

THE LOBSTER BAR

Once a wholesale fish market, this spot boasts the best lobster rolls in town, in a region that takes lobster rolls as seriously as it takes anything. Order a round of stuffies [stuffed hard-shell clams, a.k.a. quahogs] for a real Rhode Island treat. *31 Bowen's Wharf*

THE MOORING

Their seafood-fritter-filled Bag of Doughnuts is best enjoyed with a frosty beverage in hand, looking out across the water. The Grand Shellfish Platter features a whole chilled crab with an honor guard of oysters, shrimp and littlenecks. *1 Sayers Wharf*

MORI SUSHI

Sushi, sashimi and rolls galore. This casual Japanese spot is situated on Bellevue Avenue, a cheerful bit of brisk modernity amidst the neighborhood's Gilded Age bling. *181 Bellevue Ave*

FISH FEST *Stick around after summer's end to celebrate the sea's bounty at Bowen's Wharf Seafood Festival. Every October, colorful tents boast plenty of food and drink for purchase, plus free admission.*

OLD SPORT

In America's original sporting paradise, pros and amateurs can be found sharing boats, fields, courts and bar stools.

INTERNATIONAL TENNIS HALL OF FAME
Housed in historic Newport Casino. Famous for grass, hard and clay courts open to public play, and the reconstructed Court Tennis Building, where the National Tennis Club, devoted to the original version of the sport beloved by Henry VIII, still serves. A museum boasts Roger Federer hologram. Match point, metaverse. *19 Memorial Blvd*

NEWPORT COUNTRY CLUB
One of the world's most prestigious golf clubs, since 1893. Hosted the first U.S. Amateur Championship and the first U.S. Open. *280 Harrison Ave*

NEWPORT INTERNATIONAL POLO GROUNDS
Home to a series that recalls the world's first international match, played just down the road in 1886. Come for the hats and picnics, stay for the divot stomp. *250 Linden Ln, Portsmouth*

SAIL NEWPORT
New England's largest public sailing site. Rent your choice of craft and head for the open ocean, or learn to sail in the calmer harbor waters. *72 Fort Adams Dr*

CARDINES FIELD
Sandlot meets stadium, built circa 1893, thus one of the oldest ballparks in the land. Legend has it Babe Ruth and Satchel Paige played here; Yogi Berra definitely did. Currently home to the wood-bat-swinging collegiate players of the Newport Gulls. The local Sunset League, meanwhile, is one of the nation's oldest amateur hardball competitions, founded in 1919. *20 America's Cup Ave*

SURFER'S END
Wave-churning spot at the west end of Second Beach. No board? Grab a Del's lemonade and watch the wetsuits do their thing. *Hanging Rock Rd, Middletown ["between the big rock and Purgatory Chasm"]*

FIRST PLACE *Newport hosted the first X Games in 1995. For the occasion, a skate park was constructed inside Fort Adams, and a young Tony Hawk took home gold and silver medals. Search for video and ye shall find.*

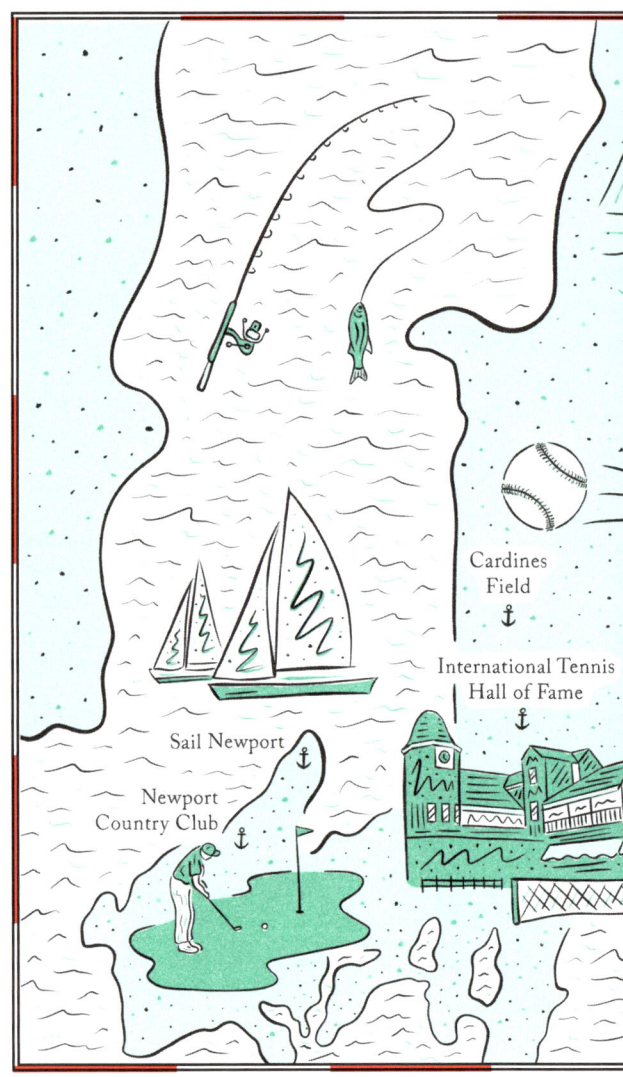

INCLUDING

060   *Audrey Finocchiaro*
062   *Kim Roberts*
065   *Nick Mele*
066   *Bill Mountford*
067   *Robert McCormack*
068   *Jesse Macrae*
070   *Patty Miller*
071   *James Brandon Lewis*
073   *Mariana Gonzalez-Trasvina*

INTERVIEWS

Nine conversations with locals of note about coffee, community, America's Cup, society photography, tennis, mansion upkeep and jazz.

INTERVIEWS

AUDREY FINOCCHIARO

COFFEE SHOP OWNER

THERE'S THE traditional sailor, preppy side of Newport. And then there's also this artistic, fun, creative side of Newport.

ONCE YOU START working in the restaurants in Newport, you're sort of there—you're a lifer.

I MOVED HOME after college and built a coffee cart in my parents' basement with my boyfriend. He was bartending; I was waitressing.

OUR FIRST EVENT was a sheep-shearing in Jamestown—hilarious.

WE STARTED NITRO because we were looking for community and a way to integrate back into Rhode Island.

COFFEE IS A great way to meet people and have a conversation.

WE'RE FRIENDS WITH everyone we work with, so we have this big community. We wanted to make sure to bring them up with us as we go—livable wages, health insurance.

EVERY RESTAURANT we'd worked in had this sort of toxic environment. We really wanted to build a place where people feel supported, loved and welcomed.

IF YOU WANT to get a vanilla latte, you should be able to do that without feeling embarrassed.

THERE'S TRULY SUCH a wide range of customers. We have a local named Tony who's in his 80s. He comes in every single morning for the special white chocolate latte that we make for him. Or a group of 60-year-olds just bitching and getting lattes and teas.

SUMMER IS WHEN Newport comes alive.

WINTER IS WHEN it's just locals. We're all enjoying the restaurants, and we're all out on the water.

GO FOR A sunset drive along the ocean, stop at Brenton Point, and it looks like the world is never-ending.

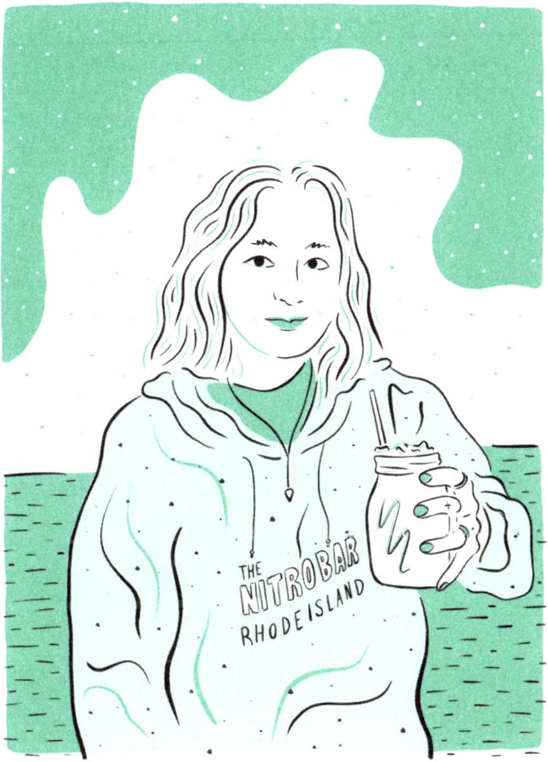
THE
NITROBAR
RHODE ISLAND

INTERVIEWS

KIM ROBERTS

SAILOR & BOAT BUILDER

GROWING UP ON Hog Island, sailing comes naturally.

BUT I REMEMBER the year that all my cousins went to sailing class and I didn't go, so I had to learn sailing from them.

I SAILED ACROSS the ocean, stopped in the Azores, up to England, and down through the canals of France to the Mediterranean.

WHILE I WAS in the Caribbean, I met Rhode Islanders. They talked about the America's Cup because it was coming up.

I FLEW HOME to visit Mom, went down to Newport and applied for a job.

I WAS AWARE of the America's Cup—slightly.

I DIDN'T KNOW anything, but I could talk the game.

I HAD TO convince them I was good enough to be part of something.

WHEN I BEGAN with the America's Cup, I got introduced to the New York Yacht Club and spent some time there. I found the yacht clubs fascinating.

I WAS MASTMAN on the *Independence* with Russell Long as the captain, and I was responsible for preparing the spinnakers: getting them ready to be hoisted, and taking them down.

THEY WANTED TO build a new boat, so my plan was to stay in Newport and build a boat.

SAILING WITH 11 people, there's no moment when everybody isn't fully busy.

IN THE AMERICA'S CUP in '83, boats sailed with 16 men.

AMERICA'S CUP would dominate the town. All the hotels would get filled. All the bars would be filled. And Ted Turner would be walking the docks.

HE WAS DRIVING *Courageous* at the time, which had already won, but the owners didn't want it anymore. And so Ted bought *Courageous* and won again.

HE HAD JUST started CNN. I thought it was the stupidest thing. Who wants to watch TV for 24 hours? I had not watched TV for a couple of years, so to me it was very strange.

NEWPORT USED TO have kings and queens walking the docks.

NOW IT'S FILLED with people who come down for the weekend and want to buy a T-shirt that says "Newport."

THE WATERFRONT has changed a lot. The stores up and down the piers change; the roads change.

I WATCH THE America's Cup, and I'm always fascinated by boat speed.

I'VE SEEN BOATS adrift, smacking into everybody.

WE HAD AN accident in the last America's Cup. Our boat flew in the air, and when it came down on the water, it broke itself, so it sank right away.

IN '83, the boat that lost the cup was called *Liberty*, and I built it.

I WAS WATCHING it on TV, and I could tell that we'd just lost the America's Cup.

"WE'RE BEHIND. Those guys are in front." And *Australia* finished in front.

THE AUSTRALIANS turned the keel upside down. They took the heaviest part of the keel and put it on the bottom of the boat. And then they added wings to it.

IT WAS A big secret. They shrouded the keel so when they hauled it out of the water, you couldn't see it. They painted it weird, so you couldn't see the shape in the water.

WE LOST AFTER 130 years.

THERE'S ALWAYS HOPE. Always good to be optimistic.

INTERVIEWS

NICK MELE

PHOTOGRAPHER

I WANT TO capture a world and a lifestyle before it completely disappears.

NEWPORT IS ONE of the last strongholds of that old-world luxury that you imagine from the 1960s and 1970s: the Slim Aarons type of lifestyle.

IT'S A PLACE that doesn't really ever seem to change that much. You go back every summer, and you feel like it's a constant.

I STARTED GETTING into photography around high school. I always had my camera with me, and realized somewhere along the way that I had a view of the world that not a lot of people got a chance to see up close.

IT'S VERY understated. People aren't driving flashy cars. There are cracks in the wall. The china has been passed down, generation to generation. People go barefoot half the time.

THE ONLY TIME your picture should appear in the newspaper is when you're born, when you're married, and when you die. Very antithetical to Instagram society.

GRAND OLD HOMES that have barely been renovated over the years. The same families own them, and they have been there for a long time.

I LOVE THE fabulous older women—these grandes dames with fantastic houses and jewelry on top of jewelry. Always a drink in their hand and a sly saying on the tip of their tongue.

GREAT HOUSES THAT are totally maximalist. Pattern on pattern. Nothing's ever taken away.

THE HOMES ALMOST say as much about the person as the person sitting in them.

YOU GO TO a party and you'll see people in tuxedos and other people in shorts without shoes. Some people are stopping by on their way to the Preservation Gala. Others are just going to go home and cook in their kitchen.

INTERVIEWS

BILL MOUNTFORD

DIRECTOR OF TENNIS

I FELL IN LOVE with tennis during the famous tennis boom.

IN THE 1970s and early '80s, our greatest champions were the big superstars of sport. It just was really attractive.

NEWPORT IS HOME to a tennis shrine: the International Tennis Hall of Fame Museum. And it's home to the original U.S. championships.

WE HAVE GRASS courts, a clay court and hard courts, six of which are indoors.

WE'RE THE ONLY public place where people can experience the wonders of getting to play on natural grass.

OUR COURTS HAVE the perennial ryegrass with a tiny bit of Kentucky bluegrass. The ball bounces firmly and high, similar to how the courts play at Queen's Club and at Wimbledon.

WHEN YOU WALK into the pro shop or you walk through the Bellevue Avenue entrance, it's almost like you're stepping back in time.

THERE'S SOMETHING very charming and wonderful about the summertime, when people dress traditionally in white clothes and play on grass courts.

THE ASSOCIATION of Tennis Professionals tournament happens every July—a major-league event in a small town.

THE ACCESS YOU get to watching players from up close here is unparalleled. It's unmatched.

THERE'S EXPERIENTIAL learning that occurs when you're playing. Knowing there are perhaps a lot of wrong ways to hit the ball, but there's no one right way to hit the ball.

WHEN I BECAME a more experienced and especially more confident coach, I knew it was better to say a lot less, but when you do speak—make sure it was meaningful.

ROBERT MCCORMACK

TOUR DIRECTOR

FORT ADAMS is an incredible, massive military structure, with history that goes back 200 years.

WE CAN EVEN kind of stretch that a little further into the Revolution, when they had fortifications here.

THE FORT NEVER came under attack.

NATURE IS DOING her darnedest to take it down, one brick at a time.

IT'S INCREDIBLE when the festivals come in. They load it in quick, and they're out about a week after the event takes place. They get a small army to help.

WE HAVE TO get in and out of the fort using ramps called "posterns." There's a postern at the south end that's large enough to put a van through at the top. But when you get to the bottom to exit, you can barely make a golf cart fit through there.

EARLY ONE MORNING, after probably being out later than he ought to have, one of the festival guys drove the van in at the top end, and got wedged into the guard rails down at the bottom.

THE FORT'S BEEN through a lot. So yeah, we can hold off a van easy enough.

I DID GET to say hi to Jimmy Buffett one time.

IT TRULY IS Newport's backyard. We often get folks who say, "I've lived in Newport my whole life, but I never went inside."

THE REENACTMENT weekends are some of the best. All the cars are gone, so if you don't look too close, it's almost like you were back in the Civil War.

THOSE GUYS ARE very passionate about what they do. When I first started, I was told to think of reenactors as actors.

SOME OF THEM can be a little bit particular, but when they get on stage, they light up.

INTERVIEWS

JESSE MACRAE

BOXING GYM OWNER

I'M ORIGINALLY from New Zealand. Newport Rugby was looking for players, so I came over to play in 2009.

I'D ACTUALLY NEVER even heard of Newport. I thought I was going to California.

NEWPORT BOXFIT is my business. I was having trouble getting work in the States because I didn't go to college or university. I didn't want to be mixing cement for the rest of my life.

I PLAYED RUGBY since I was five years old, and only just recently retired. When you stop doing something you've done your whole life, it's like a massive void; but with my body now, it's just not going to happen.

WITH BOXING, THERE'S actually less impact on the body. Maybe more on the head, but …

SOME PEOPLE GET knocked out, but that's the sport.

I TRAINED GRINDERS for the U.S. team for one of the America's Cups.

I WORKED WITH their grinders and also their skipper, Dean Barker, who's actually a Kiwi.

THE WATER IS a spiritual thing in our culture—Māori and Polynesian.

ME AND MY KIDS try to get in the water as often as we can.

I TRY TO instill a little bit of the way of our life back home with the kids.

JUST APPRECIATING the simple things like a sunset, sunrise and being able to get in the water when it's just down the road.

I LOVE THE Fifth Ward. It's a great community, and unless there's a big occasion going on, I barely leave.

NEWPORT IN THE summer reminds me of New Zealand. It's the water and the laid-back lifestyle.

INTERVIEWS

PATTY MILLER

CHIEF CONSERVATOR

I CAME TO Newport in 2014 for a summer to work on an outdoor sculpture project at The Breakers.

MY JOB NOW is the preservation and conservation of the collections—60,000-plus objects. But I don't even think of that number.

AS ANYONE IN museums will tell you, when there's a tea service, it's one "object," but to us it's 27 pieces.

ALL OF OUR houses are 120-some years old. I don't think a lot of them were meant to be monuments to the Gilded Age when they were first built. They have their aging issues.

THE BREAKERS IS unusual because it's open all year round. We do a lot of deep-clean projects in front of the public. It gives us a chance to explain to people what we're doing.

NO ONE HAS to build scaffolding to clean chandeliers at their own house.

IF YOU SIMPLY dust, as I say, where's that dust going to go? So, we have a very careful system of using low-powered vacuum cleaners and brushes.

WHEN IT COMES to our historic plaster, we do a very specialized process of propping up the ceiling, injecting a certain adhesive, and slowly coaxing the material back into place. Making sure it's secured.

BUTTONING IT, pinning it and then making it look as though we've never been there.

THE HOUSE WITHOUT any furniture, the Isaac Bell House, has an incredibly eclectic interior, and I think it stands up very well on its own without all the contents.

IF YOU'RE TALKING about a guilty pleasure, filled with the stuff of crazy Victorian dreams, it has to be Chateau-sur-Mer.

IT'S FUNNY WHEN you realize, *Oh yeah, the 19th century is my thing.*

JAMES BRANDON LEWIS

SAX PLAYER

I'M CHASING ENERGY and my most authentic self. I'm in constant pursuit of that.

I TRY TO be a student of the game. I love when athletes say that. If they're a high-caliber player, you can tell they're a student of the game. I've been that since I was a little kid.

I TRY TO learn and grow every day. Never having a sense of arrival, but always just being honest to the moment, to the time, to the experience.

I DO A lot of emotional mapping too. If I listen to a striking piece—Archie Shepp playing with Abdullah Ibrahim on "Left Alone"—what does that feel like? How can I create with that kind of feeling?

NOT NECESSARILY verbatim. How can I compose a piece of music that reaches that same sentiment?

GETTING THE opportunity to play the Newport festival—I'm not even going to front, man. I was pretty damn excited.

I'M FROM BUFFALO. I don't need a lot. Just give me a little. I don't mean that in a negative way.

I MEAN THAT I'm going to make the best of it. Getting that phone call from Newport—that vibe was kind of overwhelming.

ALL THE PLAYERS, come on, man. All the players I love and admire, all the tenor players who have played at that festival—to be a part of that lineage.

AND IN SOME ways, it's emotional. I've been living in New York for 11 years, hustling and bustling. I played with a fair amount of people. I had support over the years from Sonny Rollins.

THAT ALL MADE me feel like, *Okay, cool, I have a little to say.*

SOMEONE'S NOTICING that I have a little to say.

INTERVIEWS

MARIANA GONZALEZ-TRASVINA

EXECUTIVE CHEF

YOU CAN'T MAKE pozole for two people. You have to make it for 20.

THAT'S THE ONE dish I've always made for the people I love.

I WAS BORN in Mexico City, and I moved to Puerto Rico when I was eight. I came to Rhode Island for college when I was 18.

EXECUTIVE CHEF wasn't the plan at all. My plan was to be a pastry chef.

AS SOON AS I made the connection that culture equals food—your food comes from what your ancestors grew and ate—I knew this was how I could represent my roots in my career.

BAR 'CINO HAS always been very special because it was the first restaurant I opened. It's where I really got my stripes as a chef.

MY JAMES BEARD nomination for Bar 'Cino happened three or four days before the state shut down for COVID. "Hey, you're nominated." Then it was like, "Just kidding."

OPENING LA VECINA was out of necessity. We had the space, and because of the pandemic, we couldn't open another Bar 'Cino at that moment.

WITH LA VECINA, I wanted to express my love for Mexican food through the menu, the things that I grew up with, the flavors.

THE BURRITOS ON Wednesdays are from my sous chef's dad, who is also Mexican.

ANOTHER DISH that comes to mind is the al pastor. It's the taco of Mexico City. It's hard to get it right. Ours isn't perfect, but it's very close to it.

MY MOM ALWAYS said something to me: that if you did something with love, it would show, and if you didn't, it would show as well. So I'm glad it shows in a good way.

INCLUDED

076   **HOMECOMING**
By Ann Hood

080   **SECRET BEACH**
By Christopher Ross DeSanto

084   **FRIDAY, JULY 10, 1970**
By Shannon Ali

088   **A NEWPORT AQUARELLE**
By Maud Howe Elliott

STORIES

Essays and selected writing from noted Newport voices

HOMECOMING

Written by **ANN HOOD**

I LEFT RHODE ISLAND after college, and stayed away for 15 years. Like so many small-town girls, I never intended to return, but there I was in a U-Haul truck, the Manhattan skyline glittering behind me in the early spring light. I was eight months pregnant, and the baby's father had run off with someone else instead of marrying me on the beach as we'd planned. Like an April Fool's joke, it snowed that day as I lugged boxes and bags up the two flights of stairs to my new apartment.

Sam was due on May 1. So it came as quite a surprise when two weeks before that, at my routine check-up with my midwife, she sent me for a sonogram because the baby seemed to have stopped growing. A couple hours later, I was in the hospital being prepared to give birth. "I'm not ready yet," I told anyone who would listen. Most of my boxes still needed to be unpacked and I hadn't mastered the mysteries of the car seat yet. I hadn't even finished my birthing classes. "We don't get to decide these things," a nurse said, patting my arm.

On April 16, the baby arrived at a tiny four and half pounds, wrinkled and skinny and beautiful. The man I was supposed to marry appeared and then vanished again. A couple days later, I had a new roommate: Sam. I struggled a lot over the next few months. The stroller confounded me. Figuring out what to do with the baby when I showered was a never-ending challenge. And that car seat … How I hated that car seat, with its straps and buckles and awkward way of snapping out to become a heavy baby carrier to lug around stores.

But I triumphed too, in small, magical ways. I found a soft baby sling that Sam loved, and the two of us explored our new neighborhood that was awash in pink and white dogwood blossoms. We walked miles, the two of us, up and down Newport hills and streets lined with colonial houses and historic buildings.

I often hummed all the songs I loved on those walks: all the protest songs and love songs and heartbreak songs. I'd look down and find Sam smiling up at me. At the end of our walks, I'd sit at The Coffee Exchange with Sam snuggled close to me, sip coffee made from just-roasted beans while I read *The New York Times*, pleased with myself for finding both coffee and a newspaper. Pleased that Sam was, finally, napping.

Spring became summer—a summer so hot the candles in the candleholders on my mantle melted. One afternoon, as I sat in my stuffy apartment, Sam fussed in his bouncy seat, sweaty and cranky like me. A box fan spun warm air at us from the window. It was July and I couldn't imagine what came next for Sam and me. "Okay, buddy," I said, lifting my baby into my arms. "Let's go where there's some air conditioning." The closest place I knew that had AC was my beat-up Volvo. I got Sam in the car seat, muttering about how someone needed to invent an easier one of these things, blasted the air conditioning, turned up the radio, and started to drive south toward the beaches.

"Mark your calendars," the disc jockey said when Lovin' Spoonful's "Daydream" came to an end. "The Newport Folk Festival is August 7 and 8 this year, with John Prine, Nanci Griffith, The Indigo Girls, Joan Baez, and Peter, Paul and Mary." I memorized the phone number for the box office as the DJ shared it, repeating it over and over so I wouldn't forget.

***

As a Rhode Islander, I grew up hearing about the Newport Folk Festival. I remember when Bob Dylan went electric for the first time on stage in 1965. The festival started in 1959 as a response to the burgeoning folk music scene sweeping across the country. That first summer, on a hot Saturday afternoon in July, folk heroes like Pete Seeger and The Kingston Trio took the stage at Freebody Park. But the one who stole the show was a barefoot 18-year-old named Joan Baez, who'd been invited on stage as a guest of Bob Gibson. Together they sang two songs—"Virgin Mary Had One Son" and "We Are Crossing Jordan"—earning her the nickname The Barefoot Madonna.

A few years later, in 1963, Joan Baez joined the Student Nonviolent Coordinating Committee and 600 festival goers on a protest march past the mansions on Bellevue Avenue. By then, the festival had expanded from one day to three, and the finale on Friday night united Baez, Peter, Paul and Mary, Bob Dylan and Pete Seeger onstage for a show-stopping sendoff. They clasped hands and sang "We Shall Overcome." Joan Baez wasn't the only

STORIES

folk singer launched at the festival. She introduced Bob Dylan there in 1963. Johnny Cash had an unknown Kris Kristofferson perform "Me and Bobby McGee" at the 1969 fest. And that same year, James Taylor debuted to a standing ovation after singing "Carolina in My Mind."

***

Sam [dressed in a tie-dyed onesie], my cousin, and I set off on that hot August morning for Fort Adams. [In the years since that first fest, it had relocated from Freebody Park to Fort Adams State Park, an actual fort built in 1841 at the mouth of Narragansett Bay.] There was a sea of people, and the stage beyond, and then, in every direction, breathtaking views of bay or harbor. As we made our way through the crowd looking for a spot to lay out our blanket, I realized I wasn't just there to hear the soundtrack of my youth. I was there to rediscover that girl who'd listened to those records in her small bedroom. She was hopeful and optimistic and brave. All the things the grown-up me needed to be now.

As soon as the music began, it worked its magic. When Peter, Paul and Mary sang "Puff, the Magic Dragon," it felt like they were singing the song right to Sam and me. It's the song I'd played to him before he was born, one headphone ear piece in my ear, the other on my belly. After he was born, it became both of our favorite lullaby, me singing in my off-key voice to him the way my own mother had sung it to me.

At the final chorus, I picked up my beautiful baby boy and danced, both of us smiling as we twirled. The blazing sun was red and hot, sitting low over Fort Adams by the time Pete Seeger made a surprise appearance with Joan Baez. The whole crowd stood and sang along with them, perhaps me loudest of all. The glorious music washed over me as the voices from my past lifted me up once again.

ANN HOOD is a Rhode Island native, and author of *The Italian Wife*, *The Knitting Circle*, *Somewhere Off the Coast of Maine* and numerous other books. She has won the Paul Bowles Prize for Short Fiction, and two Pushcart Prizes.

SECRET BEACH

Written by **CHRISTOPHER ROSS DESANTO**

YOU REMEMBER a typical summer day. Grab the bike—summer's here and the tourist congestion makes the roads unbearable. Put your headphones in, but keep the music off [you'll want to hear the chorus of summer's song]. Watch the sundresses and the sunscreen-coated skin glisten in the July air. Smell the ice cream, lobster rolls and gasoline like a fanfare of summer to your slow-waking morning senses.

People wave hello here. It's the humid season now and the sun begs to see your bare shoulders. Erika waits by the path in the reeds, so you climb down the thorny embankment onto the shiny slate rocks to the spot that cuts into the Narragansett. The days are longer now and you crave sun, water, isolation, and a couple of oysters don't hurt either. Today's bounty is a clams casino that your grandmother taught you, baked last night and reheated in your kitchen. You cook better with a little sand on the linoleum.

Secret Beach tickles your hubris into thinking that here, among the purple slate and sargassum, you have a sacred piece to yourself. It feels, if even for a brief moment, that you could have yourself a home here. Your fingers smell of sweet tabasco, lemon, clam juice and pickle brine. Breathe it in. You've been making this mignonette your entire life. Today you add chives from the garden. "Tricia and Wes brought the littlenecks in from The Vineyard this morning." We know a guy.

***

I've sat here many times: Secret Beach, in all manner and stage of life. There, by the large gray rock, I squeezed 30 people on its bulging breast. We were 21, dumb and excitable. We had a large birthday feast of Italian and Portuguese foods. In the Newport way, we ate the meals of the Catholic countries whose people filled this beautiful land. Those immigrants in turn shared recipes and their tables, and added with love a new hue to our state's tapestry—a love of tinned fish, zeppole, caçoila and "Mike, where'd you put the limoncello?"

Past the gray rock, if you're bold enough to scale the spiny cliff, you'll find a secluded cove. It's narrow and dark and *damn those kids, I swear to God if they leave their bottles here again, I'm gonna kick their asses.* The mouth of that cove is the meatball sub and lemonade spot. It's a meatball sub and lemonade spot because that's all we could afford back then. The mouth of that cove is where I sat with him. We held hands. I told him I loved him. He told me he had to leave. It's the meatball sub and lemonade spot because he's a picky eater and I can't get him to eat vegetables. France was calling him back and he needed to find a piece of himself out there. Something about this island and these people haunted him. It's the meatball sub and lemonade spot because he blew all of his money on weed again. I saw an update on an app the other day that flashed brightly with news of his new marriage. On an LED screen with my brightness a little too loud, a small hand reached inside of me and clenched my throat. He looked happy, and glowing, and not the tortured soul I tried and failed to fix years ago. Though it was once hard, it's gotten easier these days to let him go, but I do thank him for our time.

And so, even if masochistically, I sit in the meatball sub and lemonade spot still. Tell me, Secret Beach. Tell me it'll be OK. No, not about him, I just ate the sandwich. I'll be alright. Tell me I can take you with me.

* * *

What do you say to the place that's held you? The place on the Atlantic that's shown you the only stable life you've known. On slate beaches in sand, you've pieced together the parts of yourself you've come to know and love. Cobblestone streets gripped your feet when love and heartbreak tossed you off balance. In hot corners of loud bars, under warm lights, you've cried and laughed and yelled with friends come and gone.

Newport: I've built a dream of a life with you in it. A slow life. Tucked away—maybe by the Fifth Ward—with a tiny plot of land, I've dreamt of a garden. But the bills and prices wake me up. I'm slapped awake by foreign license plates on luxury cars. I count the zeros added to the real estate signs, running like silt through my thin fingers. I run to the coast, but another hotel's gone up and—well, it's getting harder to find the shore.

***

And so, like always, I'm back at Secret Beach.

In a dream of mignonette, littlenecks and tautog I host small dinners over candlelight. Diving into the Grand Marnier and Fernet, we pore over life and realize we are truly one degree separated from another. It's an adage come to us Rhode Islanders to remind you that here, among the humid tourist crowd of the summer and the brooding, isolating winters, you can truly, truly belong. Here on these rocks at Secret Beach I hold the only thing I'll ever own on the island: these memories. A one-degree-separated-from-my-dream consolation prize for a luxury I was not born into. Yet, as I sit and look out into the rich grays of the water, I am not upset. I am full and satiated by the time spent here by the water. Looking down I see the belly of a man well-loved and nourished by this place: the meals and love of a life well-lived, on Secret Beach, in the sleepy town of Newport.

"Happy birthday! Heading to Secret Beach. On bike, see you in 15." Pass the bread, I haven't eaten all day. I skipped lunch again. Yeah, I know it's not healthy, but I was busy. Well, I went to the beach, came back, showered, took a nap and now I'm back here. So, yeah, I didn't have time to eat! "France sounds amazing. Will you think of me? I wish I knew how to help you." So what did you do today? Oh, nice, I gotta check that place out. No, don't go there, there's gonna be a line. It's nine o'clock are you crazy? "Thank you for the oysters, Tricia. How was fishing season this year?" Alright I'm gonna go to bed. Thank you thank you for dinner, I really appreciate it. Text me when you get home.

CHRISTOPHER ROSS DESANTO is a born-and-raised Rhode Islander living in Newport. He is an engineer, an uncle and a dinner party host.

FRIDAY, JULY 10, 1970

Written by **SHANNON ALI**

IT WAS NEARLY one week after the 70th birthday of Louis Armstrong, or so it was generally believed. His exact birth date remains unknown even now. Be that as it may, the Newport Jazz Festival devoted its globally famed stage to a celebration of the icon, a moment for jazz musicians, singers and music lovers from all over to extend their gratitude to the great "Satchmo," the man widely considered the father of this American art form.

Armstrong had been convalescing at home in New York for some time, under doctor's orders, due to heart and kidney problems. But that summer, he set out for a number of birthday tributes, first at the Shrine Auditorium in Los Angeles on July 3. He arrived early in Newport for rehearsals. To his dismay, Armstrong's All-Stars band members were noticeably absent. George Wein, the Newport impresario who had persuaded him to sign on for the festival showcase, would enlist trumpeter Bobby Hackett as musical director and bring in several then-rising stars, like bassist Larry Ridley, drummer Oliver Jackson and Jimmy Owens on trumpet.

Still, the show went on. As the tribute night neared, Armstrong's personal photographer, Jack Bradley, documented the rehearsals right up to performance day. Armstrong would receive $6,500 for the live set [equivalent to roughly $51,000 today], and agreed to have the show recorded and broadcast exclusively on NBC's popular radio program *Monitor*. While he didn't have his regular band to back him, Wein brought a little New Orleans to the festival, inviting the Eureka Brass Band and Preservation Hall Jazz Band to perform.

Hackett kicked off the night with the "Trumpet Player's Tribute." Just as the song ended, Armstrong walked on stage. It was a surprise. The audience greeted him with thunderous applause, and he began singing "When It's Sleepy Time Down South." Few jazz instrumentalists are equally compelling and palpable as singers. With Armstrong, you cannot help but stop whatever you are doing and give him your undivided attention. His gravel-tinged tenor voice mirrored the range and vibrato of his clarion trumpet cries.

The night unfolded as a musical odyssey into Armstrong's earliest influences by way of Dixieland and ragtime. The set segued into tributes from the many trumpet players Armstrong had influenced. Dizzy Gillespie took the mic and matter-of-factly said, "[I'd like to take] this moment to thank Mr. Louis Armstrong for my livelihood," before he playfully mimicked Satchmo's gravelly vocals to sing "I'm Confessin.'"

* * *

Louis Armstrong's place in history has always been complicated. While he is now widely regarded for his prowess as a musician, there were times at the height of his career when many considered him to be kowtowing and passive on issues of racism and discrimination. Behind his famous Cheshire-like grin was a highly complex man who couldn't show his vulnerability; that could only come out through music. While everyone immediately recognizes Armstrong, no one can say we ever knew who "he" was, apart from being a celebrated musician.

The musical moment surrounding the tribute was as unknowable in its own right. The '70s would soon give rise to punk, funk and disco, and an endless list of singers and songwriters. Jazz artists like Miles Davis, Freddie Hubbard and Herbie Hancock were in the midst of broadening the genre's boundaries by fusing it with rock, electronic and soul. All these developments would be considered by some to be the death of music. It all signaled a time of significant change.

The Newport Jazz Festival was also beginning to feel the musical crossbreeze. For its 1969 program, the festival booked a mix of jazz and rock acts throughout its summertime weekend, aiming to reach ever-expanding audiences. The following year, Wein would declare that the line-up would revert to a mostly jazz format, as he felt 1969 was "maybe too much rock."

On that night of July 10, one result would be an unprecedented moment in jazz history.

* * *

Like Armstrong, Mahalia Jackson's life and example embody the totality of the Black experience. Born in New Orleans as the granddaughter of slaves, Jackson broke barriers as she popularized gospel blues during a time when the ravages of Jim Crow were pervasive. Her facial expressions alone captured the gravitas of Black life—not just her own, but that of the countless Black people who were denied the promise of the American dream.

Late in the show, Mahalia Jackson joined Armstrong on stage. To see Jackson and Armstrong together at that moment was a collective embodiment of what—and where—Black music had been throughout the 20th century.

While Armstrong relied heavily on his audience while performing, an essential part of live jazz, the church is a different animal altogether. Before Jackson sang the classic hymn "Just a Closer Walk with Thee," a palpbable hush fell on the crowd, just as she prepared to "testify" before them:

"I want to dedicate a song to a great man that has given America one of the great arts of the world, jazz, this great contribution—not only America but the world.

I want to sing this song because he happens to be from my hometown. A man with a warm smile. A man that everybody loves, and if you don't love him, I don't really think you know how to love."

As Jackson opened with "Just a Closer Walk with Thee," dressed in a full-length blue gown with coiffed hair, she appeared seemingly aware she is before a live audience at a jazz festival. A few minutes into the hymnal, though, she looked as though she were in a trance, singing with her eyes closed, hair swaying on top of her head, and dancing without a microphone. The spirits had "taken over," and suddenly, the Newport audience became her steadfast crowd of parishioners.

The rain threatened to halt the performance. And while some people left the tent, others gathered or remained in their seats to witness Louis Armstrong and Mahalia Jackson together. Watching their live set over 50 years later makes it difficult to imagine that these two artists would both pass away less than two years after this performance.

For a moment, you almost forget that they are two titans of Black music standing side by side. As Satchmo warmly embraces Jackson like a little sister, they remain in an embrace while he sings an impassioned chorus, and Jackson calls out the lyrics.

SHANNON ALI [Shannon J. Effinger] has been a freelance arts journalist and cultural critic for over a decade. Her writing on all things jazz and music regularly appears in *The New York Times*, *The Washington Post*, NPR Music, *Pitchfork*, *EBONY* and *DownBeat*, among others. Born and raised in Brooklyn, she currently lives on the Upper West Side and is developing her first book-length work.

STORIES

A NEWPORT AQUARELLE

Written by **MAUD HOWE ELLIOTT**

Originally published in 1883.

"WHO IS THAT TALL GIRL with Mrs. Fallow-Deer?" "You have been in Newport twenty-four hours and don't know? Why, that is Gladys Carleton. You've heard of her, of course?"

"Can't say I have. A New York belle, I suppose, from her get-up?"

"Yes; her ambition is to be taken for an English girl, though, of course, you detected the spurious imitation of your countrywomen. At what point does the Anglo veneer fail to cover the American girl?"

"I shouldn't say she was veneered at all, but she's a typical New Yorker. I can't tell you exactly where the difference lies, but I could pick you out a New York girl from a crowd of specimen women from every town in England and America. They have a way of holding their elbows, and a certain half-arrogant, half-flirtatious, entirely fetching poise of the head, that beats all the other women in creation."

"I, being a New Yorker, thank you for the compliment. Do you think Gladys Carleton a beauty?"

"Perhaps I should if you were not here; I can hardly tell. My eyes are rather dazzled. If Miss Carleton is your friend, won't you present me to her?"

The lady addressed seemed not altogether pleased at this request, but she answered,—

"Oh yes; I will stop her when she passes back this way. I cannot leave my seat, or I shall never get another."

The speakers were seated in the long crescent-shaped corridor of the Newport Casino. The hands of the quaint golden clock on the tower of the outer courtyard pointed to the hour of twelve. It was mid-day, and all the fashionable world of Newport was gathered within the aristocratic enclosure just named. Some of the more energetic people were playing lawn tennis in the fine grounds of the inner courtyard, which separates the semi-circle of the open corridor from the theatre and racket court. Others were lunching luxuriously in the well-appointed restaurant, and a few of the more serious-minded butterflies were sitting in the comfortable reading-room, where ladies, as well as gentlemen, are admitted to read the news, and write their impressions of the place to their less fortunate friends and relatives, broiling in town or rusticating in Maine. But the great crowd of people were assembled in the open corridor, listening to the music of the band, which at that moment was playing the exhilarating strains of the "Merry War." Seated on either side was a double row of people, who laughed and chatted with each other, criticising the less fortunate latecomers who had found no seats, these last having no other resource than to walk up and down between the two rows of well-dressed men and women. The most popular of the ladies held little courts of their own at different points of the corridor, and were surrounded by circles of men, of whom they spoke to their husbands as friends, to their lady acquaintances as beaux.

The lady who had promised to stop Miss Carleton as she passed by, had succeeded in securing for herself a seat close to the steps which led down from the corridor to the tennis courts,—a veritable coigne of vantage, from whence every eligible man who passed up or down the steps could be arrested by a smile or a word. She had hurried her toilet in order to be early on the ground and make sure of the coveted spot. It was not to be wondered at that she was not in haste to surrender it, in order to oblige Mr. Cuthbert Larkington by an introduction to Gladys Carleton. She did not intend to surrender either her seat or her cavalier, for Larkington was certainly the most stylish-looking man in the whole Casino, and was, besides, sure to become the lion of the season. He had arrived in Newport only the day before, bringing a letter to Mrs. Fallow-Deer. He had been told that the only thing necessary to open all doors in that exclusive society to an Englishman was the patronage of this distinguished lady. Mrs. Fallow-Deer had a right to the high position she held in Newport society. She was by birth a Van Schuylkill, of New York, and belonged to one of the old Dutch families, who had always stood well in Manhattan, since the days when their ancestor, Peter Van Schuylkill, came out among the earliest settlers. In her youth Miss Van Schuylkill had accompanied her father to England, whither he had been sent as American Minister, and while

STORIES

there she had been sought in marriage by Mr. Fallow-Deer, an English gentleman, of large fortune. After thirty years of wedded life in the mother country, Mrs. Fallow-Deer had returned to the home of her youth, a widow, and a very rich woman. She had soon made her house in New York one of the most attractive in the city. A social leader she was born to be, always had been, and was likely to die in harness. She had certain eccentricities, but was essentially conventional in thought and conversation; she had talked so much society talk that it was impossible for her to doff her worldly manner and her social vernacular, which she carried into her most intimate domestic life. From her long residence in England, she had come to be considered by the men and women of her set as a sort of oracle of *les convenances*.

MAUD HOWE ELLIOTT [1854-1948] was an author and socialite in her own right, the daughter of abolitionist Julia Ward Howe and Samuel Gridley Howe, founder of Boston's Perkins School for the Blind. Her 1883 novel *A Newport Aquarelle* captures the essence of the city's 19th-century elite.

INDEX

INDEX

22 Bowen's 16
Aardvark Antiques 18
Agassiz, Alexander 10, 33
Age of Innocence, The 9
Ali, Shannon 88
America's Cup 34, 68
Armstrong, Louis 84
Astor, Caroline 24
Audrain Auto Museum 20
Baez, Joan 9, 25, 77
Bannister's Wharf 49
Belmont, Alva 24, 32
Benjamin's 17, 54
Benson, Nicholas 21
Big Weather Gear 18
Bit Players, The 20
Black Pearl, The 17, 55
Boom Boom Room 8, 19
Breakers, The 42, 43, 48, 70
Brenton Point 60
Canonicus 10, 37
Cara 17
Cardines Field 10, 55
Casino Theatre 19
Chart House Inn 9
Charter Books 18
Chinese Tea House 47, 48
Clean Ocean Access Team 21, 49
Clementine's 17

Cliff Walk 10, 11, 49
Codman, Jeff 21
Cottage & Garden 18
Croquet 36
Crow's Nest 17
Del's Lemonade 8, 16, 55
DeSanto, Christopher Ross 80
Dining Room at Castle Hill Inn, The 17
Dive Shop, The 18
Drawing Room, The 48
Duke, Doris 24, 26
Dylan, Bob 25, 40, 77
Easton's Beach 49
Eisenhower, Dwight 32, 33
Elliott, Maud Howe 88
Elms, The 48
Fastnet Pub, The 16
Finocchiaro, Audrey 60
Flo's Clam Shack 54
Folk 18
Fort Adams State Park 10, 55, 67, 78
Franklin Spa 17
Giusto 17
Goat Island 49
God's Little Acre 31
Goddard and Townsend 26

Golf 42, 43, 55
Gonzalez-Trasvina, Mariana 17, 73
Great Gatsby, The 9
Green Animals Topiary Garden 20
Harrison, Natasha 21
Hartnett, John 21
Hood, Ann 76
Hotel Viking 9
Humming Bird 17
Hunt, Richard Morris 48
Hutchinson, Anne 39
International Tennis Hall of Fame 36, 55, 66
Isaac Bell House 70
Island Surf & Sport 21
Jackson, Mahalia 86
Jane Pickens Theater, The 20
Kennedy, John F. 32, 33
Kiel James Patrick 18
King, Billie Jean 36
Kingscote 10, 48
Kitt Kites 19
Kristen Coates 20
La Vecina 17, 73
Lazuli Handcrafted 20
Le Bec Sucré 16
League of American Wheelmen 29
Lennon, John 27

Leno, Jay 32
Leo's 17
Lewis, Ida 27
Lewis, James Brandon 71
Lipton, Sir Thomas 34
Lobster Bar, The 54
Long, Russell 62
Macrae, Jesse 68
Mamma Luisa 17
Marble House 24, 48
Matunuck Oyster Farm 19
McCormack, Robert 67
Mele, Nick 65
Miantonomi 10, 37
Michael Hayes 18
Midtown Oyster Bar 16
Miller, Patty 70
Mitchell, Joni 25
Moonrise Kingdom 9
Mooring, The 54
Mori Sushi 54
Mountford, Bill 66
Narragansett Tribe 10, 37
New York Yacht Club Regatta 19
Newport Casino 55
Newport Classical Music Festival 19
Newport Contemporary Ballet 20
Newport Country Club 55
Newport Flower Show 20
Newport Folk Festival 9, 19, 25, 40, 77
Newport International Polo Grounds 55
Newport Jazz Festival 9, 35, 84
Newport Lobster Shack 16, 55
Newport Mercury 300
Newport Restoration Foundation 20, 24
NewportFILM Outdoors 20
Nitro Bar, The 16, 60
Norman Bird Sanctuary 19, 21
Ocean Drive 49
Omori, Kenji 21
Original Nine 36
Perro Salado 17
Preservation Society of Newport County 20
Primavera 18
Raso, Perry 21
Re-Sails 18
Redwood Library and Athenaeum 13, 20
Rejects Beach 49
Rhode Island Red Food Tours 21
Richards, William Trost 37
Roberts, Kim 62
Rogue Island Comedy Fest 19
Rose Island Lighthouse 11, 49
Royal Male 18
Sachuest Point 19, 37
Safe Harbor Newport Shipyard 49
Sail Newport 55
Second Beach 8, 55
Seeger, Pete 25, 77
Simmons Farm 19
SkyBar, The 17
Stokes, Keith 21, 31
Surfer's End 55, 57
Sweet Berry Farm 19
Taylor, James 25, 79
Thames Glass 19
Tirella, Eduardo 24
Touro Synagogue 39
TSK 8, 17
Twain, Mark 32
van Beuren, Andrea 21
Vanderbilt, Consuelo 48
Vanderbilt, Cornelius 43
Vanderbilt, The 9
Vanderbilt, William K. 24
Vonnegut, Kurt 32
Wally's Wieners 17
Washington, George 39
Weekend of Coaching, A 48
Wein, George 25, 84
White Horse Tavern 16
Wild Season Florals 18
Wilde, Oscar 32
Yagi Noodles 16
Young, Elizabeth 21